Source book 197

7

WAR CRIMES
AGAINST SOUTHERN
CIVILIANS

WAR CRIMES
AGAINST SOUTHERN
CIVILIANS

Walter Brian Cisco

PELICAN PUBLISHING COMPANY

GRETNA 2007

The word "Pelican" and the depiction of a pelican are trademarks
of Pelican Publishing Company, Inc., and are registered in the
U.S. Patent and Trademark Office.

Library of Congress Cataloging-in-Publication Data

Cisco, Walter Brian, 1947-
  War crimes against Southern civilians / Walter Brian Cisco.
    p. cm.
  Includes bibliographical references and index.
  ISBN 978-1-58980-466-1 (hardcover : alk. paper)
  1. United States—History—Civil War, 1861-1865—Social aspects. 2.
War crimes—Southern States—History—19th century. 3. Civil—
military relations—Southern States—History—19th century. 4.
United States. Army—History—Civil War, 1861-1865. 5. Whites—
Crimes against—Southern States—History—19th century. 6.
African Americans—Crimes against—Southern States—History—
19th century. 7. United States—History—Civil War, 1861-1865—
Destruction and pillage. 8. United States—History—Civil War,
1861-1865—Atrocities. 9. Confederate States of America—Social
conditions. 10. Southern States—Social conditions—19th century.
I. Title.
  E468.9.C465 2007
  973.7'1–dc22
                                    2007009386

Printed in the United States of America

Published by Pelican Publishing Company, Inc.
1000 Burmaster Street, Gretna, Louisiana 70053

For Hunter

Contents

Acknowledgments

Thanks are due the staffs of the following institutions: the University of South Carolina's Thomas Cooper Library (particularly the longsuffering folks in the Interlibrary Loan Department) and South Caroliniana Library; Library of Congress; William L. Clements Library, University of Michigan; Special Collections Library, Duke University; Robert W. Woodruff Library, Emory University; and the Huntington Library.

I appreciate, too, all those individuals who contributed material, ideas, and encouragement: Clyde Wilson, Don Livingston, Tom Elmore, Randy Simpson, Bill Moody, and David Cisco. I only wish that I could have used every piece of information given me.

This is a better book for the advice, assistance, and inspiration of others. Any shortcomings are entirely the author's.

WALTER BRIAN CISCO

WAR CRIMES
AGAINST SOUTHERN
CIVILIANS

Chapter 1

An Introduction to Lincoln's War

In the midst of his 1863 invasion of the United States, Gen. Robert E. Lee issued a proclamation to his men. After suffering for two years innumerable depredations by their enemies, some Southerners, soldiers and civilians, thought at last the time had come for retaliation. Lee would have none of that. He reminded his troops that "the duties exacted of us by civilization and Christianity are not less obligatory in the country of the enemy than in our own."

> The commanding general considers that no greater disgrace could befall the army, and through it our whole people, than the perpetration of the barbarous outrages upon the unarmed and defenseless and the wanton destruction of private property, that have marked the course of the enemy in our own country. . . .
>
> It must be remembered that we make war only upon armed men, and that we cannot take vengeance for the wrongs our people have suffered without lowering ourselves in the eyes of all whose abhorrence has been excited by the atrocities of our enemies, and offending against Him to whom vengeance belongeth, without whose favor and support our efforts must all prove in vain.[1]

Accustomed as we are in our own time to war's unmitigated horrors, the injunction of Lee seems anachronistic if not quixotic, yet is a measure and reminder of how much has been lost.

Through the centuries, by common consent within what used to be called Christendom, there arose a code of civilized warfare. Though other issues are covered by the term, and despite lapses, it came to be understood that war would be confined to combatants. Thus limited, said historian F. J. P. Veale, "it necessarily followed that an enemy civilian did not forfeit his rights as a human being merely because the armed forces of his country were unable to defend him."[2] According to Veale, the amelioration of war's barbarism did not come as a direct result of Christianity, or even from the rise of European chivalry, but "as the product of belated common sense." As early as the eighteenth century, Swiss jurist Emeric de Vattel, author of *The Law of Nations,* expressed what should be obvious to any student of history: breaking the code on one side encourages violations by the other, multiplying hatred and bitterness that can only increase the likelihood and intensity of future wars.[3] "There is today," concluded Vattel in 1758, "no Nation in any degree civilized which does not observe this rule of justice and humanity."[4]

Yet warring against noncombatants came to be the stated policy and deliberate practice of the United States in its subjugation of the Confederacy. Shelling and burning of cities, systematic destruction of entire districts, mass arrests, forced expulsions, wholesale plundering of personal property, even murder all became routine. The development of Federal policy during the war is difficult to neatly categorize. Abraham Lincoln, the commander in chief with a reputation as micromanager, well knew what was going on and approved. Commanders seemed always inclined to turn a blind eye to their soldiers' proclivity for theft and violence against the defenseless. And though the attitude of Federal authorities in waging war on Southern civilians became increasingly harsh over time, there was from the beginning a widespread conviction that the crushing of secession justified the severest of measures. Malice, not charity, is the theme most often encountered.

Lincoln's embracing of "hard war" may have had consequences more far-reaching even than defeat of the South. Union
general Philip Sheridan, in Germany to observe that empire's
conquest of France in 1870, told Otto von Bismarck that defeat-
ed civilians "must be left nothing but their eyes to weep with
over the war." The chancellor was said to have been shocked by
the unsolicited advice. But the kind of warfare practiced by the
Federal military during 1861-65 turned America—and arguably
the whole world—back to a darker age. "It scarcely needs point-
ing out," wrote Richard M. Weaver, "that from the military poli-
cies of [William T.] Sherman and Sheridan there lies but an easy
step to the total war of the Nazis, the greatest affront to Western
civilization since its founding."[5]

"In war, as in peace," observed Weaver, "people remain civilized by acknowledging bounds beyond which they must not
go." Echoing the words of Lee, Weaver understood no necessary contradiction in the term "Christian" as applied to the
profession of arms. "The Christian soldier must seek the ver-
dict of battle always remembering that there is a higher law by
which he and his opponent will be judged, and which enjoins
against fighting as the barbarian."[6]

Some assume that as long as there are wars, there will be
widespread excesses. Telford Taylor noted that the attitude of
Americans when informed of the massacre of South
Vietnamese civilians at My Lai was to discount it by saying
that such things are bound to happen. "So, too," Taylor pointed out, "are murders and robberies 'bound to happen' in our
streets, and they are likely to happen much more often if we
cease to regard them as reprehensible."[7] Others justify war on
civilians as necessary to achieve victory. They applaud the
depredations of Sherman, hail him as a man ahead of his time,
and smile as they repeat his "war is hell" mantra, not hearing
the totalitarian echo in their words.

Historian James M. McPherson estimated that fifty thousand Southern civilians perished in war-related deaths.[8]
Others place the figure far higher. Despite such numbers apol-
ogists for Lincoln's "hard war" then and now downplay the suffering endured and damage done, lay much to "mistakes" or

"accidents," or even try to place blame on victims themselves. Little attention is paid to the poor who were plundered or to brutalized African-Americans. Many cling to the Lincolnian myth that only by the most horrendous of wars could the slaves be freed, ignoring the fact that the rest of the Western world managed to bring an end to the institution without bloodshed.

But one conviction remains an American article of faith: the war on Southern civilians was justified—the war itself was just—because it resulted in saving the union.

Abolitionist Lysander Spooner spent a lifetime battling slavery, but surprisingly found little to rejoice in over the outcome of Lincoln's war.

> The principle, on which the war was waged by the North, was simply this: That men may rightfully be compelled to submit to, and support, a government that they do not want; and that resistance, on their part, makes them traitors and criminals.
>
> No principle, that is possible to be named, can be more self-evidently false than this; or more self-evidently fatal to all political freedom. Yet it triumphed in the field, and is now assumed to be established. If it really be established, the number of slaves, instead of having been diminished by the war, has been greatly increased; for a man, thus subjected to a government that he does not want, is a slave.[9]

The Deep South understood Lincoln's sectional victory in the 1860 presidential election to be a revolutionary event that virtually abolished the confederated republic of the founders. In withdrawing from the union, they simply removed themselves from a government they did not want. It took Lincoln's declaration of war five months later to convince others of his true intentions, prompting a second wave of secession. The sovereign people—organized as sovereign states—had created the federal government in ratifying the Constitution. States that entered the union of their own free will now left it in the same manner.

"The reason Lincoln gave for launching a military invasion

of the South was to save the Union,'" wrote Thomas J. DiLorenzo.

> Translating from his obfuscating rhetoric, this means that he wanted to use military force to destroy once and for all the doctrines of federalism and states' rights that had, since the founding of the republic, frustrated ambitious politicians like himself who wanted a highly centralized and greatly enlarged state.[10]

Federal troops died to preserve the union. But, Lincoln's pious poetry to the contrary, it was their opponents in gray who struggled "that government of the people, by the people, for the people, shall not perish from the earth."

The people of Maryland never had the opportunity to choose whether to remain in the United States or join the new Confederacy. The Federal army overran the state, and Lincoln was quick to jail legislators and other elected officials, close newspapers, and suppress free speech in his zeal to insure "loyalty." Lee, on crossing the Potomac in 1862, issued another extraordinary document, this directed to the citizens of that suffering state.

> Believing that the people of Maryland possessed a spirit too lofty to submit to such a government, the people of the South have long wished to aid you in throwing off this foreign yoke. . . . In obedience to this wish, our army has come among you, and is prepared to assist you with the power of its arms in regaining the rights of which you have been despoiled. . . .
>
> We know no enemies among you, and will protect all, of every opinion. It is for you to decide your destiny freely and without constraint. This army will respect your choice, whatever it may be; and while the Southern people will rejoice to welcome you to your natural position among them, they will only welcome you when you come of your own free will.[11]

That principle—of people having the right to freely choose their own destiny—was utterly repugnant to Lincoln. In waging war on civilians he returned to the barbarism of the past, but he also dealt a blow to limited, constitutional government from which America has yet to recover. That all Americans are less free today, and live in a more dangerous world, are among his legacies.

Chapter 2

"We Believe in a War of Extermination"

Keeping Missouri in the Union

As the seven states of the Deep South departed the union during the winter of 1860-61, the majority of Missourians, in common with the people of other Border States and those of the upper South, longed for an amicable settlement of differences between the sections. The state had voted for Democrat Stephen Douglas in the presidential election, Abraham Lincoln running last in the four-way race. Delegates elected to a state convention that met on February 28 to consider Missouri's course of action were overwhelmingly opposed to secession. Still, they warned against federal coercion of the South. When that convention met again the following month delegates called for compromise, resolved that Missouri remain in the union, then adjourned subject to recall.[1]

On April 15, Lincoln ordered each state to send troops so that he might invade the newly formed Confederacy. Whatever their view of events up to then—even if they believed the first wave of secession unjustified—most Southerners still in the union could not countenance such coercion. To them, denying fellow Americans their right of self-determination was simply wrong. "Your requisition, in my judgment, is illegal, unconstitutional, and revolutionary in its object, inhuman and diabolical, and cannot be complied with," replied Gov. Claiborne Fox Jackson. "Not one man will the State of Missouri furnish to carry on any such unholy crusade."[2]

St. Louis County was but one of two in the state carried by Lincoln in the 1860 election, that due to large numbers of recently arrived German immigrants. Still, in the spring of 1861 the city of St. Louis was hardly a bastion of Lincolnism. The Republican mayor and his administration were swept from office on April 1 and the president's declaration of war against the Confederacy on April 15 was widely decried. The political situation remained fluid and volatile.[3]

As required by law, Missouri militia units mustered in early May for their annual period of training and drill. Local St. Louis militiamen pitched their tents at Lindell Grove, on the western boundary of the city, under the direction of Brig. Gen. Daniel M. Frost.[4] Whatever their individual inclination, every officer and soldier in the Missouri militia had taken an oath to defend the Constitution and laws of the United States, and the Stars and Stripes flew over their encampment, called Camp Jackson.[5]

In command of the local U.S. Army garrison was Connecticut-born Capt. Nathaniel Lyon. Convincing himself that the Federal arsenal was in danger of seizure by secessionists, he had ordered most of the arms stored there be shipped to Illinois.[6] Lyon then discovered evidence that the governor was arranging with Confederates to smuggle artillery to the Lindell Grove encampment. Calling Missouri militiamen "a body of rabid and violent opposers of the General Government" and "a terror to all loyal and peaceful citizens," Lyon determined to strike.[7] But first he would augment his small force of regulars with German Unionist volunteers. Permission granted by the War Department, Lyon soon commanded between six and seven thousand men—his German recruits armed, but most without uniforms.[8] On the afternoon of May 10, Lyon marched his force through the streets of St. Louis to Lindell Grove, surrounded Camp Jackson, and demanded its surrender. Frost, outnumbered eight to one, confessed himself "wholly unprepared to defend my command" and ordered his men to lay down their arms.[9]

A hostile crowd of onlookers gathered as Lyon marched those 689 crestfallen prisoners, surrounded by their captors and led by a band playing "The Star-Spangled Banner," back through the streets of the city. It was 5:30 P.M. Outraged citizens heckled the Germans and began throwing rocks, dirt clods, and other objects at them. According to a witness, one German soldier shot into the crowd even as some fired a warning volley over their heads. Almost immediately, other German troops lowered their rifles and began shooting civilians. Some would later claim that a few in the crowd, armed with pistols, returned the fire. When it was over, twenty-eight civilians lay dead on the streets of St. Louis, a number that included two women and four children. Seventy-five others were wounded. Three of the prisoners were also killed, as were two soldiers, probably victims of stray fire by Federals. (Capt. Constantine Blandovski, for example, was mortally wounded by a minié ball—a kind of bullet possessed only by his own troops.)[10]

There was more bloodshed on May 11 as another hastily recruited German regiment was issued weapons. This time Lyon reported ten civilians killed along with two of his soldiers.[11]

Over the next few days as many as ten thousand citizens—terrified by Federal violence—fled St. Louis. Convention delegate Uriel Wright had opposed Missouri's secession but now wondered if he had been wrong. "If Unionism means such atrocious deeds as I have witnessed in St. Louis, I am no longer a Union man."

Exactly one week after the St. Louis massacre, Nathaniel Lyon's Washington superiors promoted him from captain to brigadier general.[12] Lincoln's aggressive policy was now out in the open, but it was no longer possible for Missourians to freely choose their own political future, as Lyon had marched his troops on the capital of Jefferson City. Governor Jackson and other elected leaders were forced to flee, the Union military soon overran most of the state, and a regime approved by Washington was installed. Later that year a state government-in-exile was formed that adopted an ordinance of secession, and Missouri was formally granted admission as one of the Confederate states.[13] Yet until liberation might be achieved, the people of Missouri were at the mercy of Federal occupiers.

Decrees were not long in coming from their blue-uniformed

masters. In December 1861, Maj. Gen. Henry Halleck, commanding the Department of Missouri, issued orders that those "known to be hostile to the Union" would be taxed "in proportion to the guilt and property of each individual," proceeds supposedly earmarked for "suffering" Unionists. Those assessed had one week to appeal, but if they were unable to prove their loyalty to the United States, the amount due would increase 10 percent. "Any one who shall resist or attempt to resist the execution of these orders will be immediately arrested and imprisoned."[14] Those who could not pay cash had their furniture and other property seized and auctioned, typically at a fraction of its true value.[15]

On January 1, 1862, Halleck declared that it was the responsibility of the military to punish undefined "crimes and military offenses" committed within his department. Though he seemed to realize that his order was without legal authority, the "good of society and the safety of the army imperiously demand this." Under Halleck's edicts partisans and guerrillas were denied the rights of combatants "and are liable to the same punishment which was imposed upon guerrilla bands by Napoleon in Spain and by Scott in Mexico."[16] Confederate authorities had begun commissioning officers and organizing independent companies to resist the Union occupation of Missouri, but to Halleck "every man who enlists in such an organization forfeits his life and becomes an outlaw."

Commander of the Confederate Trans-Mississippi Department, Lt. Gen. Theophilus Hunter Holmes, protested.

> Looking at these matters as calmly as the facts will admit of, I can see but one result of the course which the Federal Government and its officers are thus adopting. That result is—a war of extermination. . . . We cannot be expected to allow our enemies to decide for us whether we shall fight them in masses or individually, in uniform, without uniform, openly or from ambush. Our forefathers and yours conceded no such right to the British in the first Revolution, and we cannot concede it to you in this.

Holmes' reasoned response made no impression on Federals.

Little wonder. That year, fewer than four thousand Confederate guerrillas in Missouri were tying up as many as sixty thousand Union troops badly needed elsewhere.[17]

In order to make it easier to identify the "disloyal," a series of general orders were issued in July 1862 requiring every able-bodied man to report for duty in the "Enrolled Militia" of Missouri. Exemptions could be obtained by those willing to first join and then pay a fee, and those deemed "disloyal" were assessed huge sums to support this organization. "All arms and ammunition of whatever kind and wherever found, not in the hands of loyal militia, will be taken possession of," read General Order No. 19, forbidding citizen ownership of firearms of any kind for any purpose in the state of Missouri.[18]

Loyalty oaths and the posting of huge performance bonds to guarantee their observance became widely imposed. By this device tens of millions of dollars were extorted from Missourians. Additionally, an elaborate array of fines and assessments charged local citizens thousands of dollars whenever a Federal soldier was killed or wounded in their neighborhood or when property was lost—regardless of who might have been responsible.[19]

General Order No. 35, issued Christmas Eve 1862, required provost marshals to "arrest and take evidence against all persons guilty of disloyal conduct"; guilt was assumed prior to arrest and without any need for evidence. Jailed were Missourians "who encourage the rebellion by speaking, writing, or publishing any disloyal sentiments, or induce the same in others." Not overlooked were those who "while pretending that they are better Union men than those charged with the control of the Government, constantly denounce the Government. . . . They will be arrested, the evidence taken against them, and be proceeded against as criminals." Federal authorities would not be deterred by any difficulty in obtaining evidence. Provost marshals were to arrest "notoriously bad and dangerous men, where peace and safety require it, though no specific act of disloyalty can be proven against them; and such may be put under bonds, imprisoned, or required to leave the state."[20]

Often the authorization for arrest and exile came long after the actual persecution had taken place. In the fall of 1862 the president of McGhee College in Macon County was exiled with five other citizens to northern Illinois.[21] In November, Brig. Gen. Benjamin Loan reported on his activities to Maj. Gen. Samuel R. Curtis, his superior in St. Louis. "La Fayette [County] will require a good deal of severity before it can be restored to its allegiance," wrote Loan. "I left about 250 of the inhabitants in confinement and ordered others to be arrested. Some 50 men fled the country to avoid arrest, who will probably never return, and some 50 others gave their parole to leave the State in ten days, not to return during the war." Loan recommended that prominent individuals be arrested and held "in close confinement" out of state since that "would be a manifestation of power and determination on the part of the Government that would strike terror into the souls of these craven rebels, for most of them are cowards."[22] Curtis would himself later defend the policy of banishment, sure that it did much to promote "the success of our arms and the progress of our principles."[23]

Dr. Joseph McDowell of St. Louis was no coward. For speaking out in favor of the Confederacy, the physician had his property seized and converted into a prison by the military, one of but many they would need. Formerly a medical college and academy, what became the Gratiot Street Prison held five hundred inmates, but that number soon reached eleven hundred men and women. Overcrowding, lack of food, and filthy conditions led to outbreaks of disease that killed nearly half the prisoners one year.[24]

Lucy Nicholson Lindsay was imprisoned there. She described the warden, one Masterson, as "a horrid man." Upon her arrival, he called her a "Southern aristocrat," inquiring sarcastically, "how she'll like prison fare?" Another lady sharing the same cell suffered repeated hemorrhages of the lungs, apparently tubercular. Masterson had an officer bring her the false news that one of her children had died. "She commenced screaming and had another coughing fit," said Mrs. Lindsay, who called the Yankee a liar and condemned his cruelty. "He laughed and said, 'I just wanted to see how much grit she had.'"[25]

It was not unusual for women to be jailed in Union-occupied Missouri. In August 1862 two women from Hainesville, Clinton County, were arrested for refusing to swear allegiance to the United States. In early December, Union troops captured letters penned by Confederate soldiers from Missouri serving in Arkansas. Addressed to their loved ones at home, these letters proved a bonanza to Federal authorities, allowing them to identify the "disloyal" and target them for arrest and punishment.[26]

It took extraordinary courage to publicly voice opposition to what was going on in Missouri. Among newspapers shut down by Federal authority or Unionist violence were the *Morning Herald* and *Missouri State Journal* in St. Louis, the *Expositor* and the *Express* of Lexington, Platte City's *Sentinel* and *Argus,* the *Cape Girardeau Eagle,* the *Hannibal Evening News,* the *Banner* of Fayette, the *Border Star* of Independence, the *Carrollton Democrat,* the *Franklin County Weekly Advertiser,* the *Shelby County Weekly,* the *Columbia Standard,* the *Macon Register,* and at least seven others.[27]

By the spring of 1863, Loan decreed that only those loyal to his government might engage in business or grow crops. Eighty Lexington businessmen raced to sign a resolution proving their loyalty but were placed under arrest and had their places of business closed because they signed late![28]

In the rural areas and small towns of Missouri arson, theft, and murder became so common that vast sections of the state were uninhabited by war's end.[29] "We believe in a war of extermination," said Brig. Gen. James H. Lane. "I want to see every foot of ground in Jackson, Cass and Bates counties burned over—everything laid waste. Everything disloyal from a Shanghai rooster to a Durham cow must be cleaned out." On September 23, 1861, his artillery opened fire on the Saint Clair County courthouse. It burst into flames, and soon the rest of Osceola was blazing as well. The bank was robbed, and Lane's men downed a large quantity of whiskey. Theft went on everywhere in town, the general himself taking a carriage, piano, and supply of dresses. Lane's chaplain, Rev. Hugh D. Fisher, stole the altar furnishings from a local Osceola church, explaining that he needed the items for his own church in

Lawrence, Kansas. A long wagon train loaded with plundered goods accompanied the troops back to their Lawrence base. On November 14, 1861, Kansas cavalry commander Charles Jennison and his troopers took everything of value from the people of Independence, leaving with a similar train of spoils. According to Jennison, his was a "Self-Sustaining" regiment. Lt. Col. Daniel Anthony spent the fall of 1861 raiding in Cass and Jackson Counties. He wrote to his abolitionist father back in Massachusetts, urging that brother Merritt come to Missouri since "I could give him a chance to make money fast." Colonel Anthony bragged of all the property he had taken from the "Secesh." He was especially proud now to have four black servants waiting on him, he told sister Susan B.[30]

In January 1862 troopers of the Seventh Kansas Cavalry burned 45 buildings in Dayton, Cass County, before turning their attention to Rose Hill in Johnson County. There 42 structures were torched. The owner of one home was shot to death, and the Kansans helped themselves to livestock and wagons. Union troops in the field were expected by their superiors to take what they needed. In northwest Johnson County, troopers from Kansas set fire to another 150 homes belonging to suspected Southern sympathizers. They looted the village of Kingsville, notching the ear of one man so that "We'll know you the next time you are caught." Eight other local residents were killed by the raiders. A few days later they burned the town of Columbus. That spring another Kansas cavalry regiment burned more than 20 homes near Greenfield.[31]

Union regiments recruited in Missouri were no less brutal. Their depredations included the killing of six Southern sympathizers in Warrensburg and vicinity in March 1862. "Loyal" militia also burned houses there. Militiamen in search of Southern partisan Sam Hildebrand failed in their efforts to find him, so they burned the home of his mother and murdered his uncle. That summer five prisoners in the custody of the Third Missouri Cavalry Regiment were shot and killed "while trying to escape," according to their executioners. One of the dead was Joshua Chilton, a former state senator. Union soldiers arrested Columbus Spencer at his home in Buchanan County, then shot him a half-mile away. A similar fate awaited Dr. George W. Main. Although a native of Scotland and still a British subject, Dr. Main was arrested on August 14, 1862, as a suspected Southern sympathizer. His body was found later in the Missouri River. Unionists arrested Livingston County resident Jesse P. Clark around the same time, only to murder him and leave his body on a road. They thought he might be on his way to join the Confederate army. When five Cooper County Confederate sympathizers enrolled in the militia, as required by law, they were followed home by Union cavalrymen who killed three. Federal troops under the command of Brig. Gen. John Wynn Davidson torched every structure in Carter County near the end of 1862 on the theory that the whole county was "disloyal." In Benton County, cavalrymen took six local Southern sympathizers from the Warsaw jail, telling them they must gather firewood. All were found shot on the bank of the Osage River. William R. Green, his son David, and a neighbor named Charles Hill were arrested near Fulton by Union cavalrymen on suspicion of their having helped a wounded Confederate guerrilla. The three were killed. On July 14, 1864, Federals robbed a grocery store, stole many bottles of wine, burned homes, and then torched the Methodist church in Platte City. It was, said one of them, a "wholesome and admonitory" lesson.[32]

Union horsemen made it a practice to ride up to a home at night and pretend to be Confederates themselves in the hope that their victims would reveal similar sympathies. Those who did were immediately executed. "The ladies generally went to the door," remembered one, "for they [Federals] were in the habit of shooting down the men." Another method of exposing "disloyalty" was to search for guns or ammunition since no citizen was permitted to own these items.[33]

Reverend Payne of Clinton County was arrested and carried away by a squad of Federal soldiers. The pastor was "loved by all who knew him," said a friend. "He was a good man and a good preacher." Worried, his daughter went to army headquarters at Plattsburg. "To her pathetic appeal," said a friend, "the commander gruffly replied: 'You had better look in the woods for him.'" The daughter returned home and organized a search party from the women of the neighborhood, who found him, buzzards feeding on the dead body. A witness recounted that a few nights later,

> The same Federal soldiers went to the house of John Morris . . . [and] began beating him over the head with pistols. When almost unconscious, his gray hair matted with blood, they dragged him out of the house, with his wife clinging to him. Breaking her loose from him, they dragged him out into the yard and riddled his body with bullets.[34]

In Lafayette County a group of farmers returning from the market in Lexington camped for the night beside the road. Union soldiers fired on them, assuming they were guerrillas instead of unarmed citizens. The same thing happened to other unoffending farmers a few weeks later when they were shot at by German-speaking Federals.[35]

Yankee troops having earned a reputation for shooting first and asking questions later, it was not unreasonable for people of all political persuasions—or even those who were entirely neutral—to run when approached. Unfortunately, Federals viewed fleeing itself as an admission of "disloyalty." Two citizens were shot by members of the Second Ohio Cavalry Regiment when they bolted on seeing blue uniforms. Troopers of the Third Missouri Cavalry shot three men who tried to flee their approach. Near the village of Miami, a former judge named Robert G. Smart ran out the back door of his home when troopers of the Seventh Missouri Cavalry rode up. Though the judge was no Confederate, troopers assumed that running was an admission of guilt and gunned him down.[36]

"The military of this county are getting very careless of late," joked the Unionist editor of the *Kansas City Journal* on April 7, 1863, commenting on the widespread killings. "It can't be helped, 'accidents will happen.'"[37]

Chapter 3

"Burnt District"

Order No. 11

By the summer of 1863 the second floor of the three-story Thomas Building on Grand Avenue in Kansas City had become a Federal prison for women. Incarcerated there in August were as many as twenty-seven female inmates, all accused of aiding the Southern cause and many the family members of Confederate guerrillas. Josephine, Mary, and Martha Anderson were sisters of partisan Bill Anderson. Susan Vandiver and twin sister Armenia Gilvey had a brother serving with William C. Quantrill, and both were cousins of Coleman and James Younger, all fighting in the guerrilla cause. Mollie Grindstaff and Nannie Harris had brothers riding with Quantrill, as was the brother-in-law of Nannie McCorkle. Christie McCorkle Kerr's husband and brother served with Quantrill. Most of the girls were in their teens and none was over the age of twenty. Martha Anderson, the youngest prisoner, was but thirteen.

A general merchandise store occupied the first floor of the Thomas Building. Beneath that, in the basement, was a cell that held arrested prostitutes. Next door and sharing a common wall was a structure owned by Elizabeth Cockerel and used as a Union army guardhouse. Over time, soldiers made three large entrances through the cellar wall in order to visit the prostitutes—in the process carelessly removing weight-supporting columns. Though these facts did not come to light until months later, two witnesses swore that on August 11 girders in the cellar were observed to have sunk, leading them to believe that the building was in imminent danger of collapse. Others saw the elderly merchant, assisted by the guards, hurriedly removing stock from his store and piling it on the sidewalk.

On the morning of August 13, spirited Martha Anderson so irritated her guards that for punishment they fastened a twelve-pound ball to one ankle of the thirteen year old. A little later that morning there was a deafening roar and screams of terror as the building collapsed. When the huge cloud of dust cleared, citizens came running to see what had happened and what they might do. Cries for help were coming from the rubble. The voice of Josephine Anderson was heard pleading for someone to take the bricks from her head. Too late, rescuers found her dead. Twin sisters Susan and Armenia were crushed to death, as was Christie Kerr. One victim, known only as Mrs. Wilson, was injured and died later. Of the survivors, only Nannie McCorkle escaped unhurt, miraculously delivered when she jumped from a window. Little Martha Anderson—shackled by her jailers—had both legs and back broken and her face disfigured by lacerations.

The crowd that gathered watched in horror and growing anger as the bloody and mangled bodies were removed. Authorities feared a riot and summoned soldiers with fixed bayonets to the scene.

A rumor soon made the rounds that Brig. Gen. Thomas Ewing, Union army commander, had ordered the building undermined. To shift blame for the collapse from themselves, Federals claimed that the girls had weakened the building by digging a tunnel to escape. Apparently they did not consider how unlikely such a feat might be from the second story.[1] The truth—Union persecution exacerbated by gross negligence—was bad enough.

The death and injury suffered by the girls in Kansas City had unanticipated consequences for Lawrence, Kansas. Quantrill had been planning a raid on this notorious enemy center. "When news of the tragedy in Kansas City reached Quantrill's men in the bush, they were wild," wrote historian

Brig. Gen. Thomas Ewing

Richard S. Brownlee. "It tore the last thin covering of mercy from [their] hearts." Then, just five days later, on August 18, 1863, Ewing issued his infamous Order No. 10. Among other things, "wives and children of known guerrillas, and also women who are heads of families and are willfully engaged in aiding guerrillas," would be required to leave the state of Missouri. That order, in Brownlee's words,

> was a final blow to Quantrill's boys. Those desperate, fear-crazed young men now knew that those persons dearest to them were to be forced from their homes and banished, with little money and very few possessions, from Missouri. Coupled with the death of their women in Kansas City, Order Number Ten seemed to scream for retaliatory measures."[2]

Quantrill's raid, coming just three days later, resulted in the destruction of Lawrence and the deaths of some 150 civilian residents.

"Most of the people of Western Missouri," wrote historian Albert Castel,

> looked upon the guerrillas as their avengers and defenders. . . . Consequently they aided them in every possible way, from feeding them and sheltering them, to smuggling them ammunition and acting as spies. Even anti-Confederates assisted the partisans out of fear of reprisals. Thus in effect the Federal forces in Western Missouri were opposed by an entire people."[3]

Union forces terrorized Cass and Jackson Counties in the aftermath of the Lawrence raid. If two or more farmers were seen together out-of-doors, soldiers thought this sufficient evidence that they were guerrillas and opened fire. Attempting to defend a home from Federal intruders was the cause of many deaths. Any man found wearing new clothes was assumed to have stolen them in Lawrence and was hanged. One group of three was hanged so high that their feet swung over the head of anyone riding beneath the tree. "Don't cut them down!" read the sign posted on the trunk. Soon Ewing reported to his superior that though eighty had thus far been killed, "I think it will largely exceed 100 before any considerable part of our troops withdraw from the pursuit. No prisoners have been taken, and none will be."[4]

This was the kind of action needed to restore the union, at least in the minds of many in the Federal chain of command. A year earlier, William T. Sherman had confided to his brother, Sen. John Sherman, that the farms of "rebels" should be seized and given to immigrants from the North. "We must colonize and settle as we go south," wrote the general, giving Missouri as an example of an occupied state having an as yet unsubdued people. "Enemies must be killed or transported to some other country."[5]

On August 25, 1863, Maj. Gen. John M. Schofield recommended to Ewing that he deport every resident of Jackson, Cass, and Bates Counties, destroying or appropriating all property of the "disloyal" since "nothing short of total devastation of the districts which are made the haunts of guerrillas will be sufficient."[6] Schofield's was an unnecessary suggestion. That very day Ewing issued Order No. 11. Except for Kansas City and the larger towns, "All persons living in Jackson, Cass, and Bates Counties, Missouri, and in that part of Vernon included in this district . . . are hereby ordered to remove from their present places of residence within fifteen days." Those able to prove their loyalty to the Union could move to a military installation within the district or to any county in Kansas not bordering Missouri.[7] The territory affected made up almost three thousand square miles, with a population of more than twenty thousand, and all were about to become homeless refugees. The number uprooted was even greater than the fifteen to twenty thousand Cherokees forced to take the "Trail of Tears" in the infamous removal of 1838-39.

Most of the displaced headed to Kentucky, Tennessee, Texas, or even hated Kansas. Unionist George Caleb Bingham witnessed the scene for himself.

> Bare-footed and bare-headed women and children, stripped of every article of clothing except a scant covering for their bodies, were exposed to the heat of an August sun and compelled to struggle through the dust on foot. All their means of transportation had been seized by their spoilers, except

Order No. 11 by George Caleb Bingham (*Used by permission, State Historical Society of Missouri, Columbia*)

an occasional dilapidated cart, or an old and superannuated horse, which were necessarily appropriated to the use of the aged and infirm.

It is well-known that men were shot down in the very act of obeying the order, and their wagons and effects seized by their murderers. Large trains of wagons, extending over the prairies for miles in length, and moving Kansas ward, were freighted with every description of house-hold furniture and wearing apparel belonging to the exiled inhabitants. Dense clouds of smoke arising in every direction marked the conflagration of dwellings. . . . The banished inhabitants . . . crowded by hundreds upon the banks of the Missouri river, and were indebted to the charity of benevolent steamboat conductors for transportation to places of safety.[8]

Kansas City Unionist H. B. Bouton described what he saw. "[P]oor people, widows and children, who, with little bundles of clothing, are crossing the river to be subsisted by the charities of the people amongst whom they might find shelter."

Another viewed a road "crowded with women and children, women walking with their babies in their arms, packs on their backs and four or five children following after them—some crying for bread, some crying to be taken back to their homes." One refugee remembered that it was "dry, hot and dusty. The dust so thick on the fences a person could gather it up by the hand full."[9]

Union militia stole all they could from victims before burning their homes. Fires often spread to fields and forests, giving rise to the term "Burnt District" to describe the devastated counties.[10] "With systematic destruction," wrote Federal colonel Bazel Lazear to his wife, "the torch was applied to the one-room cabin, the clapboard house, the porticoed mansion and to the barn, the smokehouse, and all outbuildings. . . . It is heartsickening to see what I have seen. A desolated country and women and children, some of them all most naked. Some on foot and some in old wagons. Oh God."[11]

Many refugee families were stopped on the road and robbed, some even outside the boundaries of the evacuated district. "Everyday or two Yankee soldiers would unload our wagons in search of something to steal," remembered one. "They said they were hunting firearms." Mrs. P. H. Haggard described how some thirty-five Union militiamen "came swooping down . . . charging and yelling" to where she and other women and children were camped.

> The first act was to take possession of all our horses, which they led off a little way from our wagons and tied to some trees. The next thing in order was to search our wagons for contraband goods, of which they knew we had none. Then tearing the wagon sheets off, two or three men would mount the wagons and pitch trunks, boxes, and everything else they contained to the ground, bursting trunks and breaking everything breakable, scattering things promiscuously; others engaged in ransacking everything.[12]

On September 6, just days before the deadline to depart, Union cavalry descended on the Roupe farm near Lone Jack, Missouri. Called "Redlegs" for the color of their leggings, the

Kansas troopers saw that the family was loading their wagons in preparation to leave. Nevertheless, they led six men a short distance away then shot them. An elderly survivor dug a common grave, lovingly placed a pillow beneath each head, covered the bodies with quilts, and prayed with the womenfolk. The dead were between seventeen and seventy-five years old. That very afternoon the grieving family, now mostly women and children, joined tens of thousands of other homeless exiles, each with their own tragic story to tell.[13]

"The order settled the border war by cutting off the supplies of the guerrillas," said an unrepentant Ewing in an 1879 interview with the *Washington Post*. "It was approved by Major General Schofield and by President Lincoln," he continued. "General Schofield said, in a letter published two years ago, that President Lincoln, himself and myself were responsible for the order, in the proportion of our respective rank and authority."[14]

Historian Albert Castel concluded:

> Order No. 11 was the most drastic and repressive military measure directed against civilians by the Union Army during the Civil War. In fact, with the exception of the hysteria-motivated herding of Japanese-Americans into concentration camps during World War II, it stands as the harshest treatment ever imposed on United States citizens under the plea of military necessity in our nation's history.[15]

Of course the cause of the suffering of these Missourians, the reason for this persecution, was simply their desire to be citizens of a county other than the United States.

Chapter 4

"Treason Must Be Made Odious"

Oppression in Tennessee

In response to Lincoln's election, Tennessee disunionists demanded that a sovereignty convention consider the course to be taken, but voters in a February 9 referendum overwhelmingly declined even to convene such a body. Former Tennessee senator John Bell, candidate of the Constitutional Union Party, had carried his own and two other states in the 1860 presidential contest. Mountainous east Tennessee remained solidly Unionist, and a majority everywhere decried the Deep South's withdrawal to form the Confederacy. It was, after all, only an election that had been lost. Few in Tennessee even conceded that a state had the Constitutional right to secede. But on April 15, when Lincoln declared war, the political landscape changed overnight in the Volunteer State. Though Unionism persisted in the eastern region, Tennessee as a whole voted two to one for withdrawal, her governor, Isham Harris, declaring Lincoln's coercive policy "a wanton and alarming usurpation of power." And there would be no quibbling over "the abstract doctrine of secession." Exercising instead their right of revolution, the people approved a declaration of independence.[1]

Early in 1862 Federal victories opened much of the state to invasion. Nashville was occupied in late February, the first Confederate capital to fall to the enemy. Expecting eventual liberation, Sarah Polk, widow of Pres. James Knox Polk, reacted in what was in many ways typical of Confederate Tennesseans. When Ulysses S. Grant came to pay his respects she met him, reported the *New York Times,* with "a polished coldness that indicated sufficiently in which direction her sympathies ran." The former first lady made it clear that "she expected nothing from the United States, and desired nothing."[2]

Another of the invaders, a soldier from Ohio, had a dim view of those he was sent to guard. The people of Nashville were, in his words, "composed of Secesh, Niggers, and dogs, and a small sprinkle of whites."[3]

Brig. Gen. Don Carlos Buell, in command at Nashville, was of the impression that Tennesseans were essentially Unionists, and if Lincoln would pursue "a lenient course," could be quickly restored to loyalty.[4] Equally out of touch was one who should have known better, former U.S. senator Andrew Johnson, an unconditional Unionist from the eastern part of the state. Johnson was sure that a handful of secessionists had misled the majority in 1861, but with the reappearance of the Stars and Stripes most would rally to the Union. Lincoln appointed him military governor on March 2, 1862. The power given him was great,[5] but Johnson would soon realize that the task of conquering the people was even greater. "We have all come to the conclusion here that treason must be made odious and traitors punished and impoverished," he reported to his president. "I am doing the best I can."[6]

When Federal forces first set foot in Nashville, they found one United States flag already flying. It belonged to Hetty McEwen, 117 Spruce Street, who had displayed her Unionist sympathies unmolested by her Confederate neighbors since the first shots of the war. Governor Johnson held a very different view about freedom of expression. E. E. Jones, editor of the *Nashville Banner,* and James T. Bell of the *Gazette* were arrested and jailed. A dependable Lincolnite was brought in from out of state to edit the *Daily Union,* his salary paid from public funds. The Nashville Common Council, Johnson appointees all, made it illegal to speak so much as a discouraging word about the Union and labeled such talk as "seditious."[7]

The clergy of Nashville were among the first to feel

Andrew Johnson

Johnson's wrath. A group that included Methodist, Baptist, Presbyterian, and Christian Church ministers and educators was ushered into the governor's office, where he demanded they declare allegiance to the country at war with their own. When they refused, the pastors were jailed. "They are the enemies of our government," Johnson explained to the provost marshal, "and should receive such consideration only as attaches to a person guilty of so infamous a crime." Episcopal rector George Harris was arrested by military authorities and told he must "pray for the President of the United States or be hung." Harris was able to escape into exile. His church, Holy Trinity on Sixth Avenue South, was seized by the U.S. Army and used for the storage of munitions. The Methodist publishing house was commandeered for the printing of government documents. First Baptist Church was converted into a hospital before being destroyed.[8]

Persecution went on outside the capital as well. "How long, O Lord!" the Episcopal rector in Columbia, Tennessee, cried out. Soldiers had just destroyed his church's organ. They had already plundered everything of value in the sanctuary and even pried out the cornerstone of the building in hopes of finding treasure there. Clarksville's Presbyterian church was ordered closed by the military and remained so for years. In Murfreesboro the doors of every church were locked as soon as the U.S. Army came to town. Pastors there were ordered to pledge loyalty to the country invading theirs or face jail. Even to hold a funeral required permission of the authorities. The elders of Murfreesboro Presbyterian Church complained of soldiers committing "unprecedented destruction" and even of the cemetery being "desolated & desecrated."[9]

A month after Johnson took office, the superintendent of Nashville's public school system, board members, and all teachers were ordered to take the infamous oath if they intended to continue in their jobs. When they declined, the schools were closed.[10]

Nashville mayor R. B. Cheatham refused to betray the Confederacy by taking the oath and was removed from office and hauled off to prison. Elected members of the Common

Council lost their offices, and their freedom, replaced by Johnson appointees. Former governor Neill S. Brown was charged with "treason," as was James Childress, brother of former first lady Sarah Polk. Bankers Daniel Carter and John Herriford refused the oath and were jailed. Others thought to have "aided the rebellion" were arrested, sometimes at night, and held without being charged with any specific crime. Some were confined in the penitentiary, a few were transferred to Fort Mackinac in Michigan or Camp Chase in Ohio, while others were exiled. By 1863 arrests had become a daily occurrence in Nashville, leading some to wonder where they might house them all. Nearly everyone had done something for the Southern cause. One Nashville diarist sarcastically suggested that it might be more practical for the authorities to "build a wall around the city, and take out the Union men."[11]

A civilian, New Yorker William Truesdail, was brought in by the military to lead the army detective police. Truesdail's force gathered intelligence and exercised almost unlimited power over Nashville's citizens. Johnson complained that Truesdail's police were overly zealous, bringing complaints from even loyal citizens, thereby harming the Union cause.[12] The governor's major concern may have been that the detective police were under the army's control and not his own. William Rosecrans, military commander responsible for the detectives, refused to rein them in, claiming that Truesdail's critics were mostly "smugglers and unscrupulous Jews."[13]

One fall day in 1862, Dr. William Bass was leaving the Nashville home of William Harding when passing Union soldiers demanded he halt. When the doctor kept walking, they shot him. The controlled press concocted a story about his death being the result of a guerilla raid, but it soon retracted that tale when confronted with the facts. "The brutality exhibited by the Federal soldiers in this affair awakens the intensest indignation," wrote another physician. "I never witnessed its like." He went on to express surprise that military authorities did not interfere with the victim's funeral.[14]

Thousands of Tennesseans escaped the Federal reign of terror by going south. John Bell, former standard-bearer of the

Constitutional Union Party, was one of the first to flee the advance of Lincoln's army.[15] But by the second year of the occupation involuntary exile became an "effectual mode of suppressing the rebellion," in the words of Maj. Gen. Joseph J. Reynolds. "Despoil the rebels," recommended Reynolds. "Send the rebels out of the country."[16] In April 1863 a plan devised by Brig. Gen. Robert B. Mitchell, then commander in Nashville, went into effect. Those civilians who had "sympathies with the rebellion" would be forced south. A second category of individuals would be required to go north, "for the reason that if permitted to go South they might serve to swell the ranks of our enemies." If any exiled person returned, from north or south, they could expect to be executed. A third, "the most dangerous class," were to be confined in Northern military prisons.[17]

A Northern victim of political repression, former Ohio congressman Clement L. Vallandigham, appeared in Nashville on May 24, 1863. For publicly criticizing Lincoln's war he had been arrested a few weeks earlier, dragged from his home in the middle of the night, and was now being forced into exile in the South. Under guard, Vallandigham boarded a special train at the Nashville railroad station while a crowd of four thousand stood by in silent support.[18]

Soon as many as twenty-five people a day were being shipped south from Nashville. An Indiana soldier, Lt. Samuel K. Harryman, was sent to oversee one forced departure.

> I remarked that it was saddening to see a family so pleasantly situated, forced to separate, probably forever, at a time when they were situated to enjoy life together. The old gentleman began to cry, the old lady cried. The young ladies and smaller children began to gather around me weeping bitterly, and the contagion continued. I soon found the tears coursing down my cheeks.[19]

For those who were not forced to relocate, an elaborate system of taxes and assessments developed in Union-occupied Tennessee. Maj. Gen. Robert H. Milroy, guarding the Chattanooga Railroad, assessed seventy-seven "Secesh" individuals living

Tennessee "rebels" forced from their homes

in his area of responsibility for a total of $8,280. The money was meant to reimburse "Unionists" who lost property to "bushwhackers," but Milroy kept no records of disbursements.[20] A "privilege tax," along with the loyalty oath, was required of anyone doing business in Nashville. Special assessments, often huge, were made against Confederate sympathizers—supposedly to relieve the "destitute." A number of homes and businesses were simply confiscated.[21] "Those who are hostile to our Government, repudiating its Constitution and laws," said Major General Rosecrans, "have no rights under them."[22] Finally, faced with having to give up their homes and property, many began taking the Federal loyalty oath.[23] It was a tactic that had been commonly used by patriots during the American Revolution, as falsely swearing loyalty to King George III was not considered dishonorable when done under duress.

There was one form of property in Tennessee that remained

for the time untouched by Federal edict. Gov. Andrew Johnson and thirty-nine fellow Unionists signed a petition asking Lincoln to exempt the state from his Emancipation Proclamation, and the president agreed to their request.[24]

Soon after his appointment by Lincoln as Tennessee's governor, Johnson had allowed an election to go on as scheduled in Nashville for circuit court judge. There were two candidates: Unionist M. M. Brien and secessionist Turner S. Foster. Johnson was certain that citizens voting in secret and not intimidated by disunionists would put the loyal man on the bench. When Foster won by a large margin, Johnson was furious, vowing that there would be no more elections to fill local offices. Judge Foster was arrested, charged with treason, and confined in the penitentiary.[25]

A year later Abraham Lincoln gave the governor a few pointers on "reinaugurating a loyal State government," advice that by now Johnson no longer needed. "Let the reconstruction be the work of such men only as can be trusted for the Union," wrote Lincoln. "Exclude all others." Both men well understood that if free elections were permitted, the people would again choose to be free of the United States. "The whole struggle for Tennessee will have been profitless," concluded the president, "if it so ends that Governor Johnson is put down and Governor Harris put up. It must not be so. You must have it otherwise."[26]

In 1864 Johnson found himself on the ballot as Lincoln's vice-presidential running mate. Democrat George McClellan, though a Unionist, campaigned for president on a platform calling for negotiated peace with the South. Tennessee, now officially "restored to the Union," would take part in the election, though of course voting would be limited to the "loyal" minority. Still, Johnson was terrified that McClellan might carry Tennessee and issued a proclamation requiring voters to take an oath that went beyond mere loyalty. Voters in Johnson's state must "sincerely rejoice in the triumph of the armies and navies of the United States" and "oppose all armistices or negotiations for peace." His proclamation also allowed soldiers to vote in Tennessee without registration. Just weeks before the election, Union troops "yelling like demons, with loaded weapons, and charging bayonets," broke up a McClellan campaign rally in Nashville. These Tennessee Democrats twice appealed to Lincoln, begging that he protect their rights, and each time they were curtly rebuffed. In protest, they withdrew their candidate's name from the ballot. With Confederates disenfranchised and Unionists who backed McClellan sitting out the election, Lincoln and Johnson carried Tennessee by a laughable "landslide."[27]

Federal occupiers were unrelenting too in their suppression of "rebels" outside the capital. Hostage-taking was not uncommon, that tactic aimed at suppressing "bushwhackers."[28] In one attempt to identify the disloyal, Major General Milroy went so far as to order that all males age fourteen and over residing in any one of eight counties immediately enroll in the home guard. Anyone who failed to step forward would be considered an enemy "and treated accordingly."[29] The Unionist home guard already had an unsavory reputation for using their power to plunder neighbors and "settle old scores."[30]

"Not once or twice but day after day, season after season, year after year, farmers had to stand by impotently as Federal foraging squads helped themselves," wrote one historian of the situation in rural Tennessee. A soldier put a gun to the head of Rev. Jesse Cox of Williamson County, cursed him, then stole a quantity of food. The pastor prayed that "the Lord help us to bare it with patience" as Yankee soldiers forced him off his farm. "The Federal soldiers have taken every horse, mare and mule I have," recorded another Williamson County resident. "They have broken into my smokehouse repeatedly and have taken all my hams."[31] At Belle Meade, the plantation home of Mrs. William Harding, troops took or simply killed all the farm animals and stole crops. Deer and buffalo in her park were destroyed. A groom was shot, slave girls were molested, and Mrs. Harding's niece was assaulted.[32] In Robertson County, soldiers plundered the home of George A. Washington, threatened, cursed, and taunted him for two hours, then shot and wounded the old gentleman.[33] "Foraging" was what Federals called it, but one army commander admitted that "all suffer, rich and poor; of all methods of providing for any army this is the most wasteful."[34] Brig. Gen. Grenville M. Dodge was more blunt. "I propose to eat up all the surplus, and perhaps the entire crops in the country," wrote the Massachusetts native. "These people are proud, arrogant rebels" and must be made to understand "that all they possess belongs legitimately to the U.S. Government."[35]

Joe Mosely saw Confederate troops pass his home, but when Yankees came by in pursuit he refused to give them the information they demanded. He was hung three times from a tree, each time coming closer to death, still refusing to reveal what he knew.[36] On another occasion, near Sparta, citizens would not—or could not—tell blue-clad troops the whereabouts or identities of Confederate partisans operating in the region. In reprisal, Federals arrested every man in Sparta, plundered the town, "and destroyed all that could not be brought away," proudly reported their commander.[37] When Maj. Gen. George Thomas was unable to find out who had killed a number of his men, he ordered that the property of "rebel" citizens living within a radius of ten miles be assessed in the amount of $30,000. No less than $66,000 was actually collected by the general's efficient officers, and two years later the money was still unaccounted for.[38]

Soldiers guarding the railroad north of Nashville gathered up civilians whom they thought had a part in derailing one of their trains. A telegram was sent to Major General Rosecrans asking for permission "to make an example" of the prisoners. "No objection to your making an example," Rosecrans wired back, "but do not want a report. Let them fall off a log and break their necks, for instance."[39]

Troops under the command of Brig. Gen. Eleazor A. Paine charged into Fayetteville on the morning of June 15, 1864. There was the usual burning and theft, but in addition four men were arrested at random. Dr. J. W. Miller was one, a disabled veteran with a wife and small children. Thomas Massey had just left a store loaded with groceries for his family. William Pickett was singled out, perhaps because his civilian coat bore one old Confederate button. Franklin Burroughs had bounded down the steps of the Lincoln County courthouse with a license for his marriage. The ceremony was set for the next day. The four were threatened with death should no one in town volunteer information about Confederate partisans said to be operating in the area. None came forward.

As the hostages waited, John Massey asked to be allowed to take the place of his brother Thomas. "He has a wife and a young family," said John. "If you want Massey blood, take mine." Permission was granted.

"You God damned grey-eyed bushwhacking sympathizer," shouted Paine at the doctor, "I'll have you shot at three o'clock this evening with John Massey and the other damn scoundrels." But for reasons he never understood, Miller was spared.

The other three men were not. As the Yankee firing squad got ready, William and Franklin knelt in prayer. Massey grabbed them by their collars and pulled them to their feet. "Pray standing," he said. "Don't let these dogs think you are kneeling to them."[40]

Down in Franklin County sometime in late December 1864, a Unionist named Moses Pittman handed Major General Milroy a list of "disloyal" men and women, all apparently personal enemies of Pittman. Beside each name was a "narration of their crimes." Milroy went down the list, marking with his own hand "what punishment they shall suffer." By the names of Joel Cunningham and Green Denison he wrote "KILL." Next to the name of Curtis McCullum was the order "HANG AND BURN." Charlotte, the sister of Curtis, had "BURN EVERY-THING" written by her name. "SHOOT IF YOU CAN MAKE IT LOOK LIKE AN ACCIDENT," the general wrote next to the name of Cynthia, Curtis's wife. There were fifty-three other names on the list. Orders to carry out the murders and other depredations were given to Capt. William H. Lewis on January 7, 1865, with detailed supplemental instructions on destroying and plundering the property of the victims.

Milroy added the names of four other civilians in neighboring Coffee County whom he also wanted executed. Captain Lewis later apprehended three of this group, unarmed, at one of their homes. Leroy Moore and Thomas Saunders were both old men, William Saunders was only fourteen. Each had his hands bound behind his back, was forced to wade into the pond at Huffers Mill, then was shot. Only after three days did soldiers allow families to retrieve the bloated bodies from the water for burial.

On February 7, 1865, Milroy issued more orders, specifying eighteen individuals who were to have their homes and property burned. Included were the names of thirty-four he wanted shot. Four other names were listed, these to be "hung to the first tree in front of their door and be allowed to hang there for an indefinite period." The final sentence of Milroy's order read: "If Willis Taylor is caught he will be turned over to Moses Pittman and he will be allowed to kill him."[41]

Chapter 5

"Soldiers Are Not Expected to Be Angels"

Fredericksburg Pillaged

On the morning of December 11, 1862, troops of the Army of the Potomac, under Maj. Gen. Ambrose E. Burnside, began laying pontoon bridges across the Rappahannock River opposite Fredericksburg, Virginia. From streets and buildings, Confederate snipers fired on the Federal engineers, and in return Union artillery pounded the city. Finally, boatloads of assaulting troops drove back the Southerners, and the huge Union army poured into Fredericksburg on December 12. Burnside made plans to attack Robert E. Lee's army, outnumbered but entrenched on high ground to the west, the next day.

Fredericksburg is an ancient colonial city once home to John Paul Jones, James Monroe, and George Washington. Prior to the invasion, those who were able had evacuated, but some civilians—the sick, the poor—still remained. They were about to witness the first sack and destruction of an American city since the British took Washington in the War of 1812, but this time the perpetrators were themselves Americans.[1]

One resident, a little girl at the time, never forgot that day.

> From the end of the bombardment, and at the first invasion of the town by Union forces . . . Fredericksburg was mercilessly sacked. All day, from the houses, and particularly from the grand old homes that distinguished the town, came the noise of splintering furniture, the crash of chinaware, and— now and then—a scream. On the walls hung headless

portraits, the face gashed by bayonets. Bayonets ripped open mattresses and feathers heaped in piles blew about the streets, littered with women's and men's clothing and letters and papers thrown out of desks. Mahogany furniture warmed the despoilers, and ten thousand were drunk on pilfered liquors. Windows and doors were smashed, the streets full of debris, through which drunken men grotesquely garbed in women's shawls and bonnets, staggered; flames rose in smoke pillars here and there, and the provost guard was helpless to control the strange orgy.2

In truth, almost nothing was done by Federal authorities to control their men. "It seems to have been the intention of the generals to give the city for pillage," complained one chaplain, "at least no efforts were made to check them."[3] A Union soldier agreed. "No attempt was made by the officers to interfere."

Plundering of Fredericksburg

After being ordered to stack arms, his comrades were dismissed and "immediately made a dash for the houses, and ransacked them from cellar to garret."[4] An Ohioan thought it "a strange sight, a city given up to pillage. For although I heard no formal permission to plunder, yet I heard no one forbidding the men to do it."[5] When questioned about the theft and destruction going on all around him, Maj. Gen. Oliver O. Howard, supposedly a religious man, replied, "Soldiers are not expected to be angels."[6] The Episcopal church's silver communion service was stolen, and a soldier from Connecticut pilfered the pulpit Bible. The Masonic lodge was looted, and valuables from the time when George Washington was a member were taken.[7]

Three Yankee stragglers attempted to rape a local woman but were thwarted by the timely appearance of a courageous sergeant.[8]

Vandalism went on everywhere. Privates of the Nineteenth Massachusetts Infantry Regiment filled their canteens with molasses then poured the excess throughout one house. The walls of churches were scrawled with obscenities. Valuable volumes taken from private libraries became "stepping stones," laid on muddy streets to protect boots. Rifles were wiped clean with silk gowns.[9]

Henry Livermore Abbott, a rich, young, well-connected blue blood from Lowell, Massachusetts, spent his time stealing books as souvenirs for family and friends back home. "I tried to get you some memento of Fredericksburg," he apologized to his sister, "but got nothing better than a commonplace edition of Byron. I have got a very good edition of Plutarch's [L]ives for the governor. . . . I have two children's books for Frank & Arthur. I went into nearly every house to get some nice little silver thing for mamma & Mary Welch, but was too late."[10]

Abbott might have traded for something better. "In some instances," explained a Pennsylvanian, "men would enter a building, pick up an article that pleased their fancy, and after carrying it a few squares make an exchange for another piece of property."[11] Still, much plunder was simply carried outside and dropped or taken to the river bridgeheads and abandoned there.[12]

Though well-supplied by their own army, food was also stolen by U.S. troops. In one poor dwelling soldiers found only a bucket of walnuts but took it without apology. "We could go into the houses and get all the flour we wanted," bragged a soldier of the Fifteenth Connecticut.[13] A trio of hungry Pennsylvanians filled their haversacks with flour taken from a carpenter's storeroom and proceeded to build a fire to cook Johnnycakes. The cakes were too hard to bite, or even to crack apart with a knife, and it finally dawned on them that the pilfered white powder was plaster of Paris.[14]

Pianos were dragged into the streets and used to serenade revelers with "Yankee Doodle" or "The Star Spangled Banner"—before being chopped to pieces with an axe. Men in women's clothing paraded about to the amusement of their comrades. An old coach driven by a soldier in blackface was hitched to a mule. In the back were two soldiers wearing dresses, "scattering smiles and kisses to an applauding crowd" as they drove down Caroline Street.[15]

One disgusted Federal described the scene.

> The men had emptied every house and store of its contents, and the streets, as a matter of course, were filled with chairs and sofas, pianos, books, and everything imaginable. The men were beginning to make themselves appear as ridiculous as possible. Some had hauled pianos to the front doors, and were making hideous noises on them. Others in silk dresses, with beaver hat on, parading the streets . . . The shelling was a military necessity; but after the town was in our possession the pillaging should have ceased. I think our army has been disgraced to-day by this act.[16]

"The cursed Rebels brought it all on themselves by their own maddened folly," wrote another Federal, seemingly angry over the Southern effort to defend Fredericksburg.[17]

Next day, Burnside's repeated assaults against the Confederate army left over 12,500 blue-clad troops dead, wounded, or missing. It was perhaps Lee's most one-sided victory.

Despite the military triumph, as one Minnesotan observed, "the citizens of Fredericksburg are Houseless, Homeless and destitute. . . . It will be a hard winter of intense hardship for them."[18] As the Southern people rejoiced over the city's liberation, to relieve suffering they sent to Fredericksburg carloads of food and cash donations that reached $170,000.[19]

Chapter 6

*"I Shut My Eyes for
Two Hours"*

The Sack of Athens

Athens, population nine hundred, in northern Alabama's Limestone County, was described by one Illinois soldier as "a place of home-like contented beauty, a perfect garden of roses & flowers." The streets of the town were shaded by trees, the homes "large, roomy & comfortable, many of them elegant and all of them with gardens & grass plots on every side." In this spring of 1862, the unwelcome visitor concluded that "Athens is the prettiest & best looking town I have yet seen."[1]

Alabama departed the United States on January 11, 1861, but the decision had not been unanimous. A vocal minority—though appalled by the Republican triumph at the polls—remained unconvinced that Lincoln's election justified such a drastic response. Eleven days after the Alabama Convention voted for secession, a crowd hoisted the Stars and Stripes over the Limestone County courthouse, and a few days later William Lowndes Yancey, author of the Ordinance of Secession, was hanged in effigy in Athens. Over the next few weeks anger cooled. The courthouse flag came down, and citizens met to pledge their allegiance to Alabama, resolving "that we will stand by and sustain her."[2]

Lincoln's actions as president soon convinced most former Unionists of the necessity for Southern independence, and Athenians did their part to support the Confederate cause. By April 1862 the invaders had overrun northern Alabama, including Athens. Huntsville was captured and became a base of operations. But the occupying forces found themselves continually under attack by Confederate partisans. Army trains were sometimes wrecked, telegraph wires cut, supplies captured or destroyed, and Federal troops fired on from ambush. Maj. Gen. Ormsby M. Mitchel, the Union commander, claimed that these acts were committed by local citizens, people he called "marauding villains" and "plunderers."[3] It never occurred to the general that he and his men were seen as aggressors and invaders by a people who simply wished to be left alone.

A Federal troop train traveling to Stevenson was fired on in late April. The train stopped, and a Yankee captain by the name of Gates led a squad of men to a nearby house. There were no men at home. One of the soldiers approvingly described what happened next.

> While he [Gates] was talking with the women, a Sergeant went up stairs, and piling window curtains and other combustibles on a bed, set them on fire, and came down, closing the door. Soon the smell of fire alarmed the women, but the Captain strove hard to quiet their fears, until it could no longer be concealed, when he quietly remarked, "I guess the house is on fire," and walked away.[4]

When another army train was shot at a few days later, Col. John Beatty, regimental commander of the Third Ohio Infantry, stopped at the town of Paint Rock and gave the people an ultimatum. He swore that "every time the telegraph wire was cut we would burn a house; every time a train was fired upon we should hang a man; and we would continue doing this until every house was burned and every man hanged between Decatur and Bridgeport." Then, to show them he meant business, the colonel ordered little Paint Rock burned.[5]

On the first of May, the First Louisiana Cavalry Regiment, though under strength and outnumbered, galloped into Athens, scattering the Yankees and sending them scurrying back toward Huntsville.[6] Shots were fired from houses at the fleeing Federals.[7] Confederate troopers had been given vital intelligence on the occupying force by people in Athens, who then helped chase the enemy away. Mary Fielding, a twenty-nine-year-old Athens resident, wrote in her diary that "the citizens rejoiced to see them go, & to see our soldiers come in." The liberated townspeople applauded and "cheered for Jeff Davis and the Southern Confederacy," said an Ohio soldier.[8]

The freedom of Athens would be short-lived. The Confederate cavalrymen did not have the numbers needed to hold the town, retreating after they loaded wagons with captured weapons and ammunition.[9] As Federal troops prepared to leave Huntsville and move on Athens, an excited General Mitchel was heard to say that they should "annihilate" the enemy, hoping they would "not leave a grease spot" or "a post standing." An Illinois captain thought "he intended we should clean things out generally."[10]

The man who would accomplish that task was Col. John Basil Turchin, commanding the Eighth Brigade. Born Ivan Vasilievitch Turchaninov forty years earlier in the Cossack region of imperial Russia, he barked orders in a heavy accent. Turchin graduated from military school and entered the army of Nicholas I, where he helped crush a Polish uprising and assisted in suppressing Hungarians. The young officer's views were apparently liberal by Russian standards, and after Alexander II came to the throne, seeing little hope of Russia's reform under the new Tsar, Turchin and his wife immigrated to America in 1856. A supporter of the new Republican party, Turchin was given command of the Nineteenth Illinois Infantry Regiment when war came in 1861.[11]

Men of the Eighth Brigade reoccupied Athens on May 2. "Our troops were in an ugly mood," said an Illinois soldier. When convinced that Confederates were indeed gone, Turchin ordered the men to stack arms in the middle of town. "I shut my eyes for two hours," he said to the assembled infantrymen. "I see nothing."[12]

The business district of Athens was hit first. D. H. Friend's jewelry store was broken open and robbed of three thousand dollars in silver and other valuables. George R. Peck's store was cleaned out, his iron safe broken open, and almost five thousand dollars stolen. The safes in at least two other places of business were also cracked and their contents taken. Everywhere merchandise disappeared—either stolen or simply destroyed. At R. C. David's store, according to a report, troops "destroyed a stock of books, among which was a lot of fine Bibles and Testaments, which were torn, defaced, and kicked about the floor and trampled under foot." At Allen's drugstore "a set of surgical, obstetrical, and dental instruments," along with other stock, was smashed or carried away. John Malone's law office was vandalized.[13] A report, hastily compiled by citizens the next day, estimated damages at nearly fifty-five thousand dollars.[14]

One drunken soldier wandered about the town dressed in stolen finery, complete with vest, new boots, stovepipe hat wrapped in a brightly colored ribbon, "and a striped pigeon-tailed coat far too big for him." All the while he belted out "The Girl I Left Behind Me."

"Everything of value was carried out of dry goods stores, jewelry stores and drug stores," remembered Indiana sergeant George H. Puntenney. "The sacking of Athens has often been condemned," he concluded, but "was about what those Athenian rebels deserved."[15]

Residential Athens was not spared. At the home of Milly Ann Clayton, troops opened every trunk, drawer, and box, stealing what they wanted and destroying the rest. They threatened to shoot Miss Clayton, calling her "a God damned Liar" and "Bitch" when she told the intruders that she had no weapons. Soldiers then barged into the kitchen, where they attempted to rape a servant girl. Everywhere in town furniture was smashed, pianos chopped to pieces, carpets maliciously ruined, books torn, and clothing scattered. Watches, silver, and jewelry were, of course, stolen. At the Hollingsworth residence, cursing troops fired shots at the house and threatened to burn it, terrifying the pregnant Mrs. Hollingsworth. She lost the child, and she herself died. On the outskirts of town, the home of Charlotte Hine was ransacked for food and valuables. A blue-clad gang then invaded the slaves' quarters and raped a black girl. At the plantation of John Malone, outside of town, troops went to the slaves' quarters and there, too, committed rape. When one black woman dared charge a soldier with the crime, his commanding officer tried to hush it up, commenting, "I would not arrest one of my men on Negro testimony." Theft, vandalism, and assault went on all day and continued for days to come.[16]

When word of what had happened at Athens reached Maj. Gen. Don Carlos Buell, a man who frowned on atrocities against civilians, he relieved Turchin of brigade command, sending him back to his regiment. Turchin resigned his commission, but Buell refused to accept it. Instead, there would be a court-martial beginning July 7 and continuing throughout most of the month. The presiding officer was Brig. Gen. James A. Garfield, a future president of the United States.[17] At the beginning of the trial Garfield confessed to being horrified at "the ravages and outrages" committed at Athens, "sacked according to the Muscovite custom."[18] But as time progressed, Garfield was one of many who came to side with Turchin. "The more lenient we are to secessionists the bolder they become,"[19] testified Turchin, blaming his own superiors for treating rebels "tenderly and gently." "Until the rebels are made to feel that rebellion is a crime which the government will punish," concluded Garfield privately, "there is no hope of destroying it."[20] Still, the facts in the case could not be denied, and the court found Turchin guilty "of conduct prejudicial to good order and military discipline." He was sentenced to dismissal from the army, though the court recommended clemency.[21]

Buell wanted to carry out the sentence but did not have the last word in the matter. Just as the court-martial began, Mrs. Nadine Turchin, the colonel's wife, took the train for Washington, D.C. There she met with President Lincoln to plead her husband's case. Colonel Turchin had already been nominated on June 20 for promotion to the rank of brigadier general. In the midst of his court-martial, Turchin's name went to the Senate for confirmation, where he was approved on July 17 by a vote of twenty to eighteen.[22] In no uncertain terms, Buell had been put in his place. Turchin, with the blessing of

Lincoln and his Republican Senate, would return to active duty as a general officer.

The *Chicago Tribune* enthusiastically defended Turchin during the trial, editorializing that he "has had, from the beginning, the wisest and clearest ideas of any man in the field about the way in which the war should be conducted." In the aftermath of his promotion, the newspaper sponsored a huge demonstration at Chicago's Bryan Hall for the new general. Turchin, a man who had the full confidence of his president, was praised as one "who comprehends the malignant character of the rebellion and who is ready and willing to use all means at his command to put it down."[23]

"I don't see any use in trying them for what they did here," concluded Athens diarist Mary Fielding, "twill be done again all over the South where they have the power."[24]

Chapter 7

"Fleurs du Sud"

New Orleans Under Butler

After defeating forts that guarded the city, on April 25, 1862, Union warships reached New Orleans and Adm. David G. Farragut demanded surrender of the now undefended metropolis. During those negotiations a detachment of marines went ashore, hoisted a United States flag over the mint, and quickly rowed back to their ship. The sight was too much for William B. Mumford. The forty-two-year-old New Orleans resident, described as "a fine-looking man, tall, black bearded," climbed to the roof and ripped down the hated banner. He was assisted by three other men, and to the cheers of the crowd the flag was torn to shreds.[1]

It had been a gallant gesture, but nothing could now stop the Yankee occupation. Within days U.S. troops garrisoned the city, and on May 1, Maj. Gen. Benjamin F. Butler took charge of the Confederacy's largest city. A native of New Hampshire and long a resident of Massachusetts, Butler owed his rank to politics, having never commanded troops in battle. His first act was to establish martial law, though the elected mayor—stripped of authority—would retain his title.[2]

Butler soon commandeered three fine homes for himself and staff.[3] An Englishman, William Watson, described the general's reign.

> To the Custom-house he was driven daily in a splendid carriage, surrounded by a numerous mounted body guard, and

Maj. Gen. Benjamin F. Butler

with more pomp and display than I have ever seen accorded to a European monarch. He then sat in imperial dignity in his judgment seat . . . bedecked with all the feathers and tinsel that could be crowded into a major-general's uniform . . . and pronounced sentences according to his undisputed will on the unfortunate wights who were daily brought before him. To see such autocratic power vested in such a man, and the lives and liberties of so many thousands in his hand, and subject to his whim and caprice, seemed to me to be strangely anomalous in a nation which had so long borne the name of being the great seal and home of human liberties.[4]

Another British visitor observed that "the Northern Conqueror is hated cordially by every class of residents."[5] The women of New Orleans, defiantly loyal to the Confederacy, took every opportunity to express their loathing of the occupying troops.[6] In retaliation, Butler issued General Order No. 28 on May 15.

As the officers and soldiers of the United States have been subject to repeated insults from the women (calling themselves ladies) of New Orleans, in return for the most scrupulous non-interference and courtesy on our part, it is ordered that thereafter when any female shall, by word, gesture, or movement, insult or show contempt for any officer or soldier of the United States, she shall be regarded and held liable to be treated as a woman of the town plying her avocation.[7]

If Butler's order was meant as a slap in the face to the unconquered women of New Orleans, to many it seemed to imply more than that. Classing these ladies as prostitutes could be construed as license for rape, and a firestorm of criticism ensued. The mayor protested the order and was arrested.[8] Confederate general P. G. T. Beauregard had it read to his troops, exhorting them to "drive back from our soil those infamous invaders of our homes and disturbers of our family ties."[9] Louisiana governor Thomas O. Moore issued a proclamation meant to stiffen the resolve of his people.[10] Even the British prime minister, Lord Palmerston, expressed shock as he condemned the order before Parliament.[11] South Carolina diarist Mary Chesnut referred to Butler as a "hideous cross-eyed beast,"[12] and that was certainly how her countrymen saw him.

The general more than earned the sobriquet "Beast" Butler when he ordered William Mumford put to death for flag desecration. Despite numerous appeals for mercy, including one from the condemned man's sobbing wife Mary, Mumford was hanged in front of the mint on the morning of June 7.[13] Butler's supporters insisted that with the execution, "friends of the Union had an assurance that, at length, they were really on the stronger side. Order *reigned* in Warsaw."[14]

Butler issued decrees worthy of a czar. Newspapers were strictly censored, some were closed, and one was taken over by the occupiers. Arms were confiscated. Those who refused to swear allegiance to the United States were forced out of business. One man who refused to trade with Union soldiers was arrested, exiled, and had his property confiscated. Eventually Butler branded thousands of Confederate holdouts as "registered enemies" of the Union and forced them into exile. If more than three people met together on the streets of the city they risked arrest. In city schools, Southern teachers were fired and their textbooks banned. One man foolhardy enough to cheer for Jefferson Davis was sentenced to three months at hard labor.[15] An elderly doctor was imprisoned for privately criticizing Butler's "Woman Order." Anne Larue was one of several ladies imprisoned on barren Ship Island, off the Mississippi coast, for displaying Confederate flags on their clothing. "The prisons of New Orleans," reported one of Butler's victims, "are crowded with citizens whose highest offense consists in the expressions of opinions and hopes of the success of the Confederate cause."[16]

A case that drew special attention was that of Mrs. Philip Phillips. Wife of a prominent Jewish lawyer and former congressman, and mother of nine children, Eugenia Levy Phillips was a loyal and outspoken Confederate. One described her as "a fiery partisan, possessed of a superior intellect, a sharp tongue, and a decidedly demonstrative manner . . . plainly a lady, and a kind-hearted lady too." She had been on her balcony smiling and laughing during a party for the children and failed to notice the funeral procession for a Federal officer passing by on the street below. Arrested for "disrespect," Eugenia Phillips was sentenced by Butler to two years of close confinement on Ship Island. After some months there she was released, though still not allowed to return to her home.[17]

Butler's edicts even infiltrated the sanctity of the church. The Episcopal Church admonished the faithful to pray for those in civil authority, including the chief executive of the land, and such a prayer was part of their liturgy. For those under Butler's occupation, it was obviously no longer permissible to pray publicly for the president of the Confederate States of America. Nor were the Episcopalians of New Orleans, though now behind enemy lines, willing to pray for the president of the country warring against them. So, when that part of the service was reached, the Reverend Charles Goodrich simply invited members of his congregation to pray silently. Noisily demanding that public prayers be offered for Abraham Lincoln, one out-of-uniform Federal officer rudely ended a service and brought the matter to Butler. The general ordered Reverends Goodrich, W. T. Leacock, and William Fulton arrested and sent to a military prison in New York and had their churches placed under Federal chaplains. When another church burned "accidentally" one windy night, some suspected Butler's involvement.[18]

Though not allowed to openly support the Confederacy, residents of the Southern city did find ways to covertly express their sympathies. New Orleans artist J. B. Guibet created a handsome lithograph he called *Fleurs du Sud,* which was soon framed and on display in countless homes around the city. The discerning eye could discover in the colorful floral arrangement the Stars and Bars of the Confederacy, though it took Federal authorities months to figure out why the seemingly innocuous print had become so popular.

While quick to punish New Orleanians for supposed infractions of his rule, Butler's discipline of his own men often seemed curiously lax. For example, on June 10, 1862. Cpl. William M.

Chinock raped an African-American woman named Mary Ellen De Riley. Found guilty by a military court for the crime of rape, Chinock was reduced from corporal to private and fined forty dollars. In another case, it was determined by the court that Capt. S. Tyler Reed fired his pistol at an African-American boy by the name of William Bird, "hitting said Negro in the eye, destroying the eye." On that same August day the captain shot at, but missed, two other individuals. His sentence? "That Captain S. Tyler Reed be reprimanded by General Butler."[19]

"Colonel" Andrew Jackson Butler, civilian brother of the general, enjoyed extraordinary business success in New Orleans. "With plenty of capital and credit in his own and his brother's name," wrote one historian, "'Colonel' A.J. Butler led the parade of speculators who gathered like vultures in lower Louisiana." Under the Federal Confiscation Act, property belonging to Confederates—whether personal, real estate, rice, or cotton—was seized and auctioned at a fraction of its true value, reaping tremendous profits for well-placed "investors." Andrew Butler also operated a fleet of nine river-boats engaged in a profitable trade with Confederates behind their lines, under the authority of passes signed by General Butler. "Persons seeking special favors from the general," wrote a Butler biographer, "had a greater likelihood of success if they first spoke to Andrew, who charged a handsome 'fee' for discouraging his brother from confiscating their property." It was also understood that those imprisoned might be released if they talked to the colonel and if "the money was right." Though the charge that he personally looted silverware (earning him the nickname "Spoons") may have been untrue, Maj. Gen. Benjamin Butler's dealings in New Orleans netted him an estimated $2,850,000 during his tenure as the city's dictator. Brother Andrew garnered at least $3,000,000 for himself.[20]

In December 1862, Butler was transferred and given command of the two-corps-strong Army of the James. Later it was discovered that several of the general's potentially incriminating record books had disappeared.[21] His replacement was Maj. Gen. Nathaniel Banks, who soon received a letter from Andrew

Butler proffering a bribe of one hundred thousand dollars "if you will allow our commercial program to be carried out as projected previous to your arrival in this Department, giving the same support and facilities as your predecessor." Banks declined the offer, writing to his wife of the situation he inherited. "Our affairs have been terribly managed here. . . . Everybody connected with the government has been employed in stealing other people's property. Sugar, silver-plate, horses, carriages, everything they could lay hands on. . . . Our people must give up stealing, or give up their country, one or the other."[22]

During 1862 a number of Southern newspapers and individuals placed bounties on the head of General Butler,[23] though he managed to escape justice. After the war his political career was crowned with election as governor of Massachusetts. Butler is distinguished, however, as the only Federal commander branded by the Confederate government as a criminal. For "repeated atrocities and outrages"—particularly his execution of Mumford—a declaration was issued in Richmond.

> Now, therefore, I, Jefferson Davis, President of the Confederate States of America, and in their name, do pronounce and declare that the said Benjamin F. Butler to be a felon, deserving of capital punishment. I do order that he be no longer considered or treated simply as a public enemy of the Confederate States of America, but as an outlaw and common enemy of mankind, and that in the event of his capture the officer in command of the capturing force do cause him to be immediately executed by hanging.[24]

Chapter 8

"Randolph Is Gone"

Law and Order and Sherman

> For the next year and a half and beyond, the conflict waged across the fields, forests, swamps, and hamlets . . . split communities, districts, and families and set the fragments against each other. . . . Crops and houses were destroyed, as was anything of value that could not be carried or driven off. The ebb and flow of the . . . conflict had everything to do with the rise and fall in fortune of the conventional armies of the two sides. Its mainstay, style of fighting, and option of immediate resort, however, was first and foremost guerrilla warfare.[1]

A description of the Civil War behind the lines in Missouri or Tennessee? No, the author is describing the situation in South Carolina's backcountry during the American Revolution. Generations of Southerners had been raised on stories of gallant American partisans battling the British tyrants for their freedom and independence—and enduring atrocities from the likes of "Bloody" Banastre Tarleton. Daring men such as Francis Marion (the "Swamp Fox") and Thomas Sumter (the "Gamecock") became legendary heroes of the patriot cause, admired for their mastery of irregular warfare. It was not only in the South, but in the middle states as well, where partisan militia proved their value against British regulars and Hessian mercenaries. "Without these militia soldiers, and without Washington's exploitation of their capabilities," concluded one historian, "the leaders of the United States would have found it difficult to wage war for eight years against the military power of the British empire."[2]

Patriots fighting the invaders from behind the lines, using hit-and-run tactics, this was the example of their Revolutionary War ancestors that Confederates quickly adapted to their own struggle for independence. United States authorities failed to see parallels between themselves and the British but would adopt measures to suppress the insurgency that surpassed the redcoats in brutality. That William Tecumseh Sherman was prominent in that effort a few incidents from the fall of 1862 will demonstrate.

On September 23, Confederate guerrillas operating in an area controlled by the Union army tried to capture the steamboat *Eugene* as it docked at the Mississippi River town of Randolph, Tennessee. The effort failed, and apparently no one was injured. "Immediately I sent a regiment up with orders to destroy the place," reported Sherman three days later. "The regiment has returned and Randolph is gone."[3]

The following month Southern partisans armed with a twelve-pound howitzer fired from the Arkansas bank of the Mississippi, near Needham's Cut-off, just south of the Missouri state line. Their targets were the steamboats *Continental* and *J.H. Dickey*. In a protest letter to Confederate major general Thomas C. Hindman, Sherman claimed that no troops were on board, but in the same paragraph he admitted that "a reserve guard" was present and complained of being out of patience with "men who fire from ambush upon soldiers." Though Arkansas was outside his area of command, Sherman sent troops to the neighborhood to "expel ten families for each boat."[4]

In a letter written to a civilian on October 22, Sherman expressed his rising anger over another incident of partisan rangers attacking his boats. "God himself has obliterated whole races from the face of the earth for sins less heinous," claimed the general. Federals would not "chase through the canebrakes and swamps" after those responsible, "but will visit punishment upon the adherents of that cause which employs such agents." That same day orders were issued for the destruction of buildings in neighborhoods used by guerrillas. Sherman concluded with these words: "The people at large should be made to feel that in the existence of a strong Government, capable of protecting as well as destroying, they have a real interest; that they must at once make up their minds or else be involved in the destruction that awaits armed rebellion against the nation's will."[5]

"For Sherman, God had long ceased to be governor of this war," observed one scholar. "Sherman's religion was America, and America's God was a jealous God of law and order, such that all those who resisted were reprobates who deserved death."[6]

Maj. Gen. William T. Sherman

Hindman, in late September, wrote to Sherman about Lieutenant Tolleson, a captured Southern officer slated to be executed by Federals as a guerrilla. Hindman pointed out that Tolleson belonged to a cavalry company raised under Confederate authority and promised that a Wisconsin lieutenant held as a prisoner of war would be hanged in retaliation should Tolleson be harmed. Sherman replied at length, complaining of "guerrillas or partisan rangers without uniform, without organization except on paper, wandering about the country." Sherman maintained that captured guerrillas would only be executed after a fair trial, and only when that punishment was individually approved by the U.S. president. Having proclaimed his government's high standards of justice and resolute intentions, Sherman (and the Wisconsin lieutenant) escaped the dilemma with the announcement that Tolleson "escaped last week through the negligence of a guard."[7]

Writing from Jackson in November, Confederate lieutenant general John C. Pemberton brought up the murder of a civilian by Federals. William H. White of De Soto County, Mississippi, lived on the Hernando and Memphis plank road, thirteen miles from Memphis. On or about September 11, 1862, troopers of the Sixth Illinois Cavalry Regiment, assuming the young man was a partisan, shot him in the presence of his mother and wife. "White was not a Confederate soldier, not even a guerrilla, and some contend he was a good Union man," replied Sherman, admitting that "his killing was unfortunate." But to Sherman, White's death was the fault of Southerners themselves for having "torn to pieces the fabric of our Government so that such acts should ever occur." Furthermore, Sherman informed Pemberton, the killing was a civil issue, and "what shadow of right you have to inquire into the matter I don't see."[8]

Meanwhile, in neighboring Marshall County, the work of the Union army went on. "The news from Holly Springs is that the last house in the town was burned night before last," an Illinois soldier wrote home. "Pretty rough, but I say, amen. It's pretty well understood in this army now that burning Rebel property is not much of a crime." From Waterford, Mississippi, he reported that his comrades were even stealing from blacks, "and many of them are learning to hate the Yankees as much as our 'Southern Brethren' do." He continued, "The army is becoming awfully depraved. How the civilized home folks will ever be able to live with them after the war, is, I think, something of a question. If we don't degenerate into a nation of thieves, 'twill not be for lack of the example set by a fair portion of our army."[9]

Chapter 9

"Their Houses Will Be Burned and the Men Shot"

Tyranny in Tucker County

On April 17, 1861, two days after Lincoln declared war on the Confederacy, Virginia's sovereignty convention called for secession, subject to approval by a popular vote set for May 23.[1] When that day came, Virginians, by a majority of 86 percent, voted to leave the Union. The tally in seventy-five counties was unanimous, or nearly so. The 14 percent of voters wishing to remain in the union was concentrated in the western portion of the state, but even there only eighteen counties failed to register a majority in favor of secession.[2]

By summer of that year Federal forces had overrun the northwestern part of the state, and a Unionist rump regime was promptly put forward as "the Restored Government of Virginia." In October a referendum was held—with United States troops stationed at polling places to keep loyal Confederates from participating—that called for the creation of a breakaway state called West Virginia. The U.S. Constitution requires that before a new state is formed from an existing one the state effected grant its approval, so the "Restored Government" was called on to make the transaction legal. West Virginia would be admitted to the United States on June 20, 1863, retaining slavery, though committed to gradual emancipation. Fifty counties were chosen by Unionists for inclusion based on military, political, economic, and geographic considerations.[3] The will of the people was not consulted or considered. Half the counties within the boundaries of West Virginia had voted to abandon the Union in the May referendum.[4] One of those counties was Tucker, where voters endorsed secession by a two-to-one margin.[5] In the fall of 1862 the people of that mountainous western county, now behind enemy lines, waited helplessly as their future was determined by outsiders.

Their present master was a United States brigadier general by the name of Robert H. Milroy. Milroy, forty-six, was a native of Indiana, lawyer, veteran of the Mexican War, and for years a militant abolitionist.[6] Back home, his neighbors were aware of his temper. Only a year after joining the Rensselaer Presbyterian Church he was disciplined for "having resorted to unscriptural and unchristian means to avenge himself," but he promised to "refrain from similar acts of violence." Finally, his unorthodox beliefs led to suspension of church membership. Indianans knew him as a staunch Unionist, one of the first to call for volunteers to assist in "crushing out this rebellion."[7] In late November 1862, Milroy issued an edict that made his name well known North and South.

Some Unionists in occupied western Virginia were suspected of selling their horses in Pennsylvania then of making reimbursement claims with Federal authorities back home on the grounds of having been robbed by "bands of guerrillas."[8] Milroy's solution was to begin assessing Tucker County citizens for these supposed losses. On November 27 and 28, between thirty and forty people were served with papers and required to appear before the general at his headquarters in the town of Saint George. Abraham Parsons was assessed $340.00, his son Job Parsons $14.25, and Adam Harper $285.00.[9] Other amounts ranged as high as $700.00. All those "taxed" by Milroy had three days to pay, after which time he directed that "their houses will be burned and themselves shot and their property all seized." Milroy ordered his officers to "be sure that you carry out this threat rigidly and show them that you are not trifling or to be trifled with."[10]

In the same order to his subordinates, Milroy demanded that should civilians observe Confederate soldiers approaching a Federal camp, "they must dash in and give you notice." If noncombatants failed to perform as required, "their houses will be burned and the men shot."[11]

Adam Harper, eighty-two years old and crippled, avoided Milroy's death penalty by paying the assessment. Abraham Parsons and others did the same. An estimated six thousand dollars was taken by Milroy from little Tucker County. Job Parsons, probably not a land owner himself and having less property to lose, rode away to join Confederate forces commanded by Col. John D. Imboden, operating nearby.

The colonel dashed off a letter to Pres. Jefferson Davis, enclosing the summons that Milroy had served on Job Parsons. "This is only one of a thousand barbarities practiced here in these distant mountains," wrote Imboden to his commander in chief. "Oh for a day of retribution!"[12] Davis forwarded the letter to Robert E. Lee with instructions that he question Milroy's superiors, threatening "retaliation to repress the indulgence of such brutal passions" should Washington fail to respond.[13]

Two days later additional Milroy edicts came to the attention of Richmond authorities. On December 20 the general ordered that all civilians under his command take an oath of allegiance to West Virginia (a state that did not yet exist) and to the United States. Those failing to do so would "forfeit all right to the protection" of his army. From Moorefield in Hardy County, a Milroy underling issued his own threatening *pronunciamento* the same day, adding that in addition to forfeiting "protection," the recalcitrant must provide supplies for his troops. Since he was defending "the only truly republican Government in the world, rebel sympathizers, aiders, and abettors, seeking its destruction, must be made to feel the strong arm of Government, whether found in arms against it or at home with their families."[14] The people of Hardy County, like those of Tucker, had voted in May 1861 to withdraw from the jurisdiction of that "strong arm of Government."[15]

Milroy's actions could not have been unknown to his superiors. A copy of his infamous November order had been published on Christmas Eve 1862 by *The Crisis*, a Northern "peace Democrat" newspaper.[16] The General Assembly of Virginia branded Milroy an "outlaw" and offered one hundred thousand dollars for his capture. On January 10, 1863, Lee wrote to Maj. Gen. Henry Halleck in Washington, demanding an explanation for Milroy's threats of death and destruction. Should a response not be received in ten days, wrote Lee, the Confederate government "will be compelled to protect its citizens by the immediate adoption of stern retaliatory measures." Lee then penned a letter to his own secretary of war requesting that prisoners taken from Milroy's command not be exchanged, but be held for now as hostages.

Halleck told Lee he would investigate the matter and that if Milroy's orders were to prove genuine, they were "disapproved." Halleck went on to boast that United States forces had "not only observed the modern laws and usages of war," but also had patiently refrained from exercising "severer rights." Confederates, Halleck claimed, had committed "innumerable violations of the rules of civilized warfare," and he closed his letter by condemning Lee's "unbecoming threats of barbarous retaliation."

Halleck's disavowal of Milroy's orders took nearly two weeks to reach Tucker County. There would be no telegraphic communication to instantly put a stop to Milroy's confiscations and death threats. Lee's letter, with Halleck's comments, was forwarded to Headquarters, U.S. Eighth Army; from there to Headquarters, Defenses of the Upper Potomac; then to Headquarters, Cheat Mountain Division, where two weeks later Milroy could finally see it for himself. There was no promised investigation. Milroy was never reprimanded. Nothing else was said or done by Federal authorities.[17]

Lee wrote his own letter to Imboden cautioning the colonel against any retaliation on Union sympathizers in his region of command.[18]

Chapter 10

"The Best Government the World Ever Saw"

Milroy Rules Winchester

Winchester, in Frederick County, had a prewar population of 4,403, with nearly as many of her black residents free as slave.[1] In the May 1861 referendum on Virginia's secession, the county had voted 81 percent "yes."[2] Repeatedly invaded and then liberated during the first year and a half of war, on Christmas Eve 1862 began an occupation by Federals that would last for six long months.

Their conqueror was Brig. Gen. Robert H. Milroy, Republican, abolitionist, and staunch foe of all enemies of the Union. Milroy was thrilled by what he called "the most important event in the history of the world since Christ was born"—his president's recent Emancipation Proclamation. "Our boast that this is a land of liberty has been a flaunting lie," the general told his men. "Henceforth it will be a veritable reality." Some of his troops were less enthusiastic. "I never intend to stay here and risk my life for these damned niggers," wrote a Pennsylvanian.

Civilians under Milroy's sway certainly came to question the general's concept of "liberty." In a January 1863 letter to his wife, Milroy told her that "my will is absolute law—none dare contradict or dispute my slightest word or wish . . . both male and female tremble when they come into my presence . . . I feel a strong disposition to play the tyrant among these traitors."[3] Virginians had, after all, dared bear arms against—in Milroy's words—"the best government the world ever saw."[4]

Maj. Gen. Robert H. Milroy

Milroy ordered clerks to read all civilian mail, and if a word was detected that questioned the Union—or Milroy—the offending citizen could expect to be exiled. Exile or jail awaited anyone who might "insult" a blue-clad officer. When boys throwing snowballs accidentally hit one such officer, the child was arrested. It became an "illegal assembly" for as many as two people to meet publicly in Winchester. Cornelia McDonald recorded in her diary that "even the little school girls are dispersed if more than two stop to talk on the street on their way home." Another local diarist, Laura Lee, wrote that "Gen Milroy told a girl the other day, when she went to him to ask for a pass, that Hell was not full enough of rebels yet, and would not be until more of these Winchester women went there."[5]

A more serious matter was Milroy's use of what were known as "Jessie Scouts," Union soldiers dressed as Confederates. They would go to the doors of Winchester homes at night, begging for something to eat or a place to stay. Those who offered to help a man they thought a fellow Confederate faced arrest or exile. Mr. and Mrs. Lloyd Logan discovered the true identity of a "Jessie Scout" and ejected him unceremoniously from their home. The family was immediately exiled, not allowed to pack clothing or possessions. A Logan daughter, though ill, was even forced to leave her medicine behind.[6]

Milroy employed detectives clad in civilian clothing to spy on the people, eager to "report what the women talk about or if the children play with Confederate flags," recorded diarist Cornelia McDonald. One young schoolteacher, in a note to a friend, expressed an opinion critical of the general. She was taken several miles outside Winchester and simply dropped by the side of the road to fend for herself. Her school was closed.[7] Milroy's undercover agents also would loiter around stores, on the lookout for anyone attempting to make a purchase without a permit.

Smuggling food through Union lines became for some the only way to survive, as did an illegal trade with individual soldiers occupying Winchester.[8] Firewood was in short supply that winter, so Federal troops demolished every outlying fence and wooden building for that purpose.[9] Several residences in town and buildings such as Winchester Academy and the Quaker church were also converted into fuel.[10] When one woman went to Milroy's headquarters to beg for feed for her livestock, he began screaming at her. "You all brought on this devilish rebellion and ought to be crushed and deserve to starve with the cows!" Despite the fact that a declaration of loyalty to the Union would bring relief, not a single person took the oath under Milroy.

Winchester was not the only town to feel the wrath of the occupier. Berryville, Strasburg, and Front Royal were repeatedly raided. Arrests were made, and Milroy's troops robbed the "disloyal" and destroyed their property. "The way of the transgressor is hard," the general explained to his wife. "If they could not afford to renounce treason they must suffer on as they need expect no favor."[11]

When word reached Winchester of the death of Thomas J. "Stonewall" Jackson, ladies created black crepe rosette badges and wore them on the shoulder of their dresses in tribute to the fallen Southern general. Diarist Laura Lee recorded that one lady was accosted by a soldier who said that the mourning symbol "was an insult to their soldiers and must come off, and he put out his hand and tore it off her dress." Women were threatened with arrest and exile should the display continue, but one African-American lady would not be deterred. She wore the badge in public and was ordered by Federals to leave Winchester and not come back.[12]

On March 10, 1863, Milroy was promoted to major general, a commission that was to date from the previous November 29,[13] a date-of-rank coinciding with—and arguably in explicit recognition of—those draconian assessments that first brought him to prominence.

In mid-June, at the Second Battle of Winchester, Milroy and his men were routed by Confederates under Lt. Gen. Richard S. Ewell. With the Confederate flag again raised over Winchester, "citizens seemed perfectly wild with joy, many old ladies and gentlemen rushing out on their porches in their night clothes," wrote a soldier, "while children and young girls shouted and hurrahed until their strength failed them."[14]

Chapter 11

"Swamp Angel"

The Shelling of Charleston

On August 21, 1863, Maj. Gen. Quincy Gillmore, commanding Federal forces besieging Charleston, demanded that if defenders did not immediately abandon Morris Island and Fort Sumter—amounting to a suicidal withdrawal—he would open fire on the city. Even before Confederate general P. G. T. Beauregard received the note, two-hundred-pound, eight-inch-diameter shells began arcing toward the city from a distance of four miles. The first exploded in the early-morning darkness, destroying a house on Pinckney Street.

"Among nations not barbarous," protested Beauregard, "the usage of war prescribes that when a city is about to be attacked, timely notice shall be given by the attacking commander, in order that non-combatants may have an opportunity for withdrawing beyond its limits." Crossing the lines under a flag of truce, the British consul attempted to make his own complaint to Gillmore but was rebuffed. The bombardment of Charleston would continue for another year and a half.

The first projectiles were fired from a huge, iron Parrott gun mounted on a framework of logs floating on the marsh just inland from Morris Island. Dubbed the "Swamp Angel," this rifled behemoth burst after discharging but thirty-six rounds, its powder charge having been dangerously increased. Soon a Federal battery of four guns was under construction on a tiny piece of dry ground surrounded by marsh called Black Island.

Firing on the city began with regularity in November and increased dramatically after the first of the year. Assisted by additional artillery, during one nine-day period in January no fewer than 1,500 shells fell on the city. Later, a single gun nearby threw 4,253 missiles into Charleston before it burst.

The initial target was the steeple of St. Michael's Church, and though that house of worship was often hit, most projectiles exploded randomly in the lower section of the city. Incendiary shells proved defective, but high-explosive rounds started fires too. When Federals spotted smoke, they made it difficult for those attempting to extinguish the flames by quickly throwing in more shells. Once, the engine of the Phoenix Company exploded under a direct hit. The free blacks who made up Charleston's force of firefighters struggled heroically to protect their city and its people.

From the first night of the shelling, many residents began moving beyond range of the guns—some abandoning the city altogether. It is not known how many civilians were killed or injured, but many near misses were remembered. Newspapers reported a shell piercing the roof of a home, passing through a bed where three children slept, then exploding on the next floor. Miraculously, no one was hurt.[1] Forest Gibbs, a free black man, was resting after work in his Tradd Street home when an iron projectile smashed through one wall and out the other, leaving him and his family terrified but uninjured.[2]

On Christmas Day 1863, William Knighton, eighty-three, and his sister-in-law were sitting in front of the hearth in his home when a shell came crashing through the roof. His leg was shot off below the knee, and a fragment of the same projectile crushed his sister-in-law's foot. Within a week both had died from their wounds. The Christmas Day shelling of Charleston was the heaviest thus far, making it obvious that the bombardment had no military purpose, but was meant to strike terror into the civilian population. Gillmore admitted as much. "No military results of great value were ever expected," he told his superiors, though "the results were not only highly interesting and novel, but very instructive."

In the fall of 1864 it came to the attention of Federals that about six hundred Union prisoners of war were in Charleston. They were held at several locations and, compared to their compatriots at other Southern prisoner-of-war camps, lived in a degree of comfort that they well appreciated. In retaliation, for exposing these men to their own bombardment, Federals placed a like number of Southern prisoners on Morris Island, where they were subject to being hit by Confederate fire. Rather than allow this to continue, the Confederate captors transferred their Federal prisoners to inland prisons safe from the shells that continued to rain down on Charleston's women and children.[3]

Northern editors were delighted with news of the destruction, one reporting that "block by block of that city is being reduced to ashes."[4] Charleston native Henry Timrod, writing in the *Daily South Carolinian,* admitted that noncombatants who chose to flee the bombardment had been able to.

> But that which proves the ineffable meanness of the enemy, is, not that he has done these things, but that he has done them without the slightest compunction, and gloated over the supposed sufferings of the defenceless inhabitants. . . . [T]he Yankee commander, and his whole nation with him, exult in the ruin which they imagine they have been able to accomplish upon terms so cheap.[5]

When Federals became convinced that the area south of Broad Street was thoroughly demolished, gunners shifted their aim to the steeple of St. Philip's Church. That structure received at least ten direct hits, forcing the congregation to join others worshiping out of range. Finally, the Second Presbyterian Church above Calhoun Street, the extreme distance that could be reached by Union guns, was targeted.[6] Unexploded (but potentially deadly) rounds were still being unearthed in that vicinity more than a century later.

During the course of the Union shelling, from August 1863 to February 1865, as many as twenty-two thousand projectiles fell on the city.[7]

"Should you capture Charleston," wrote U.S. Army chief of staff Henry Halleck to Maj. Gen. William T. Sherman in

December 1864, "I hope that by some accident the place may be destroyed, and if a little salt should be sown upon its site it may prevent the growth of future crops of nullification and secession." "I will bear in mind your hint as to Charleston," he replied. But as Sherman thought the city already wrecked by the shelling, and since he looked "upon Columbia as quite as bad" in regards to fostering rebellion, that general would, when the time came, turn his attention to South Carolina's capital.[8]

Chapter 12

"I Intend to Take Everything"

Banks Raids Louisiana

By March 1863, Federal forces were besieging Confederates on the Mississippi River at Port Hudson, Louisiana. Soon, however, Maj. Gen. Nathaniel Banks turned his attention westward, launching a campaign in the Bayou Teche region. After taking Brashear City, Union troops in mid-April pushed back outnumbered Southern defenders at Fort Bisland and Irish Bend.

Banks promised to protect civilians, but instructions to do so were almost entirely unenforced and ignored.[1] One of the first victims of the invasion was John M. Bateman, a planter who lived on the lower Atchafalaya River. Fretting for his own safety, the seventy year old had taken the oath of allegiance to the Union and now waved his papers and pleaded for protection as a loyal citizen of the United States. No matter. His home was thoroughly vandalized, windows and mirrors broken, tableware and china shattered. Whatever soldiers could find of value, virtually everything portable, was carried away.[2]

French citizen Louis Francois Desire Arnaud tried to protect his home and property by displaying the flag of his native land, but to no avail. Yankee soldiers took everything that caught their eyes—including his wife's wedding band—smashed the furniture and china, and even poisoned his well by throwing dead farm animals into it. After they left it took months of hard work to make repairs, and Arnaud planted a crop of corn and yams. When the Union army returned in the fall of the same year, the Frenchman was desperate to avoid further theft and destruction. He immediately went to military headquarters and swore an oath of allegiance to the United States. But when he returned home he found his crops being harvested by Federal foragers. Losing his temper, Arnaud began shouting at them and was soon bound, gagged, under arrest, and sent to a military stockade.[3]

Men of the Twenty-first Indiana Infantry Regiment came ashore from a gunboat to raid the home of Dorsino Rentrop. The old man was gravely ill, and soon after the raiders departed he died. When Federals returned the following day, they arrested Rentrop's two grieving sons under the false assumption that they must be Confederate soldiers. The deceased Rentrop's grave was later broken into by Yankee robbers, forcing the family to disinter the body and return it to their home for protection. Soon both sons did indeed don Confederate uniforms.[4]

The Second Rhode Island Cavalry Regiment pillaged the home of Davisan Olivier. Troopers plundered his armoire and closets and shared among themselves the contents of his wallet. At the residence of Louise Fusilier a cavalry detachment dismounted, rushed through her front door, and began taking what they wanted. Her terrified gardener, an old man who spoke only French, was pistol-whipped by a sergeant who knocked him to the ground before going through his pockets. Mr. and Mrs. Antoine Goulas were both robbed at gunpoint and saw their infant's clothing and bedding stolen as well. A party of Federal officers grabbed watches and jewelry from the family of Joseph Frere before breaking open bureaus and armoires in search of apparel.[5]

One woman peeked through a window as the invaders marched by. She was startled "when, suddenly, as if by magic the whole plantation was covered with men."

> In one place, excited troopers were firing into the flock of sheep; in another, officers and men were in pursuit of the boys' ponies; and in another, a crowd were in excited chase of the work animals. . . .
> They penetrated under the house into the out-building,

and went into the garden, stripping it in a moment of all its vegetables, and trenching the ground with their bayonets in search of buried treasures.

John Lyons, former steamboat captain, was now a planter living on the upper Atchafalaya. A band of soldiers led by a disgruntled Unionist arrived at his home in the middle of the night and murdered him.[6]

Federal brigadier general William Dwight, Jr. confessed the crimes of his men, decrying their lack of discipline and the "utter incompetency of regimental officers." Dwight described depredations committed as the army marched from Indian Village to New Iberia.

> The scenes of disorder and pillage on these two days' march were disgraceful to civilized war. Houses were entered and all in them destroyed in the most wanton manner. Ladies were frightened into delivering their jewels and valuables into the hands of the soldiers by threats of violence toward their husbands. Negro women were ravished in the presence of white women and children.[7]

Two miles from Jeanerette an elderly man named Say, though he spoke only French, begged for protection. The nearby home of his married daughter had already "been sacked even to the destruction of his granddaughter's toys," said one Federal officer. Though he was promised a guard, "the whole plantation rang for the rest of the evening with the cackling of chickens and geese, the squealing of pigs, and the lowering of cattle," continued the officer. "The plundering went on under our noses while an order was being composed to forbid it." The guilty soldiers were admonished with a "lecture" and sent on their way.

Dasincourt Borel, living near New Iberia, lost everything to the Federal marauders, then had the audacity to complain in person to the commanding general. He at least wanted his one horse returned. "It is the only means of support I have left me," he told Banks, "and if I do not get it, I cannot support my family. My children will starve." "The horse is no more your property than the rest," replied Banks. "Louisiana is mine. I intend to take everything."[8]

The Catholic church in New Iberia was plundered as troops danced in priestly robes. The men and boys of that town were forced at bayonet point to labor for fifteen days on earthwork defenses, by order of Brig. Gen. Stephen Burbridge.[9]

It was in New Iberia that smallpox made its appearance in the invading army. Local physicians begged for vaccines that they might inoculate those unprotected among the civilian population. Their medical provisions were in short supply. At St. Martinville, soldiers of the 114th New York Infantry Regiment broke into the drugstore belonging to Eugene Duchamp, stealing or destroying all the medicines and medical instruments. Dr. Sabatier, a St. Martinville physician, swore that the vaccine eventually given him by Federal authorities was poisonous or contaminated, since in hundreds of patients it caused terrible infections that took months to treat.[10]

At Fausse Pointe, fifty-two-year-old Pierre Alexandre Vuillemot was robbed and his house plundered. He heard his wife crying for help and ran to her assistance, finding that a soldier had injured her finger in biting and then wrenching a ring from it. Another stole her ear pendants, tearing away the end of an ear in the process. As they left with their plunder, one Yankee fired his pistol at Mr. Vuillemot and at his home but fortunately in his haste hit no one. The homeowner was himself later arrested for having attempted to "assault" a Union officer.

A band of Yankees surrounded the residence of Cesair Deblank and his wife, "and employing every means that ingenuity could devise to inspire terror," one reported, "drew from the aged couple their hoarded wealth." Mrs. Deblank, emotionally overcome by the invasion of her home, died soon afterward. Narcisse Thibodeau, almost eighty years of age, was dragged from his Breaux Bridge home. Yankees beat him with sticks until he told them where his money was hidden. David F. Sandoz, living near St. Martinville, was robbed by one party of Federal troops. Then another band arrived in the night to demand money. When told he had none, they said they would search his ransacked house and shoot him if they found any. "You may search," replied Sandoz, "and I will abide the consequences." Mrs. Sandoz was threatened by cocked pistols placed against her head but stood as firmly as her husband until the thieves finally gave up.[11]

Fr. Ange Marie Jan, Catholic priest in St. Martinville, was beaten by Federal troops—kicked and struck with the flat side of their sabers. Months later, after that army fell back, St. Martinville became for a time neutral territory between Union and Confederate lines. One Sabbath morning, after services at the Catholic church, civilian worshipers gathered on the streets to socialize. For no apparent reason, Yankee soldiers on the opposite bank of the Teche suddenly began firing rifle volleys into the town. One old man, Alexandre Wiltz, fell mortally wounded. Miraculously, no one else was hit.

A resident of Vermilionville described the invasion of his neighborhood.

> The road was filled with an indiscriminate mass of armed men, on horseback and on foot . . . while to the right and to the left, joining the mass, and detaching from it, singly and in groups, were hundreds going empty-handed and returning laden. Disregarding the lanes and pathways, they broke through fields and enclosures, spreading in every direction that promised plunder or attracted their curiosity.[12]

Lt. William H. Root, of the Seventy-fifth New York Infantry Regiment, claimed that an effort was made to protect "every house of more than two chimneys," though securing them proved ineffective in practice. The lieutenant noted that "the smaller houses of the poor are left unguarded."[13] It hardly mattered. One reported that "this destroying spirit . . . spared neither rich nor poor." Buildings of all description were dismantled and used by Federals for the construction of bridges or to provide tent floors. Many were simply torched, their owners evicted. It was a common sight to see troops warming themselves or cooking over campfires of burning, plundered furniture.[14]

A variety of animals—horses, oxen, ponies, cattle, sheep— were rounded up and penned in the town of Opelousas and there left to die uncared-for. Elise Thibodeaux, living on the

Vermilion, was shocked to see hundreds of cattle corralled in his yard and then shot down by soldiers. He spoke only French and was unable to question them but concluded that the slaughter was done simply to deny the people their means of living. When neighbors came later to help bury the festering carcasses, they counted seventeen hundred dead animals. At another plantation Yankee soldiers broke the backs of calves with heavy clubs and threw sheep and pigs onto their bayonets. Newborn colts were killed. Fields, gardens, orchards, and shade trees, even ancient oaks, were destroyed. Piles of farm implements could be seen: plows, cultivators, shovels, and hoes along with coopers', carpenters', and blacksmiths' tools of every description. "In all cases," went the report, "the wood work has been consumed by fire, and the iron parts bent or broken."[15]

Arrests of civilians were common and in most cases arbitrary. Dr. Francis Mudd, a Vermilionville physician, was arrested at his home and taken to Federal headquarters. There he found several other local civilians also detained without charges. Thirteen days later all were released, only to discover that their homes had been plundered. Alexander Mouton, former Louisiana governor, was arrested and held in New Orleans for six months. There were many others.

Confederate scouts shot Union captain Howard Dwight near Bayou Boeuf. In retaliation, Banks ordered the arrest of all male citizens living on the bayou for a distance of forty miles. Sixteen were arrested in St. Landry alone. Some were mere boys. The oldest, eighty-year-old Jesse Andrus, was taken fifty-five miles from his home before being released. The others spent four days in the Opelousas jail before being transported by rail to Algiers then New Orleans. Hiram G. Roberts, forty-six, and Solomon Link, fifty, died during confinement. Finally, after two months, the rest were released and allowed to find a way home.[16]

Rev. James Earl Bradley, a young Methodist minister, lived in the home of Collin Adams, west of Opelousas. The Adams household was visited by the Yankees during their spring 1863 invasion, when the family lost a horse, a saddle, and a quantity of food. "They examined the cabins," wrote Reverend Bradley, "robbed us of our dinner (and robbed) the Negroes too. It was such fun to see a big darkie in the cabins daring white soldiers to search him." When the invaders returned in October of that year, the situation became much worse. As a Union cavalry unit rode up, Reverend Bradley raised his arms, prayed out loud, and admonished the invaders to obey the commandment against stealing. They pushed the preacher away and "began a pillage that the Devil himself would blush at." Indignant, Reverend Bradley wrote a letter of protest to the Federal commander and delivered the missive himself. Within hours he found himself under arrest "as a suspicious and dangerous character."

The home, barn, and store of Samuel Schmulen were looted and burned. He and his children managed to carry the ill Mrs. Schmulen to safety, placing her on a mattress in the yard as flames consumed their residence. Benjamin George, a fifty-year-old slave who lived nearby, saw the situation and tried to help his neighbor at least save the store. The effort was in vain. Then a group of drunken soldiers surrounded George, demanding to know why he, a black man, would try to assist this white Southerner. They demanded his money, and when George pleaded that he did not have any, one of the soldiers shot him in the right thigh. He survived the wound but was crippled for life.[17]

Banks' two invasions during 1863 accomplished little militarily. In the spring of the following year he launched an expedition against the Confederate stronghold of Shreveport, Louisiana, that came to be known as the Red River Campaign. Once again he would fail to achieve his objective, though civilians in the path of the army would suffer as never before. "From the day we started on the Red River expedition," wrote one Federal in his diary, "we were like the Israelites of old, accompanied by a cloud (of smoke) by day, and a pillar of fire by night."[18] Federals issued orders and in one case even offered a reward aimed at stopping "indiscriminate marauding and incendiarism, disgraceful to the army of a civilized nation."[19] It went unheeded.

On April 24, 1864, Confederate major general Richard Taylor reported on the situation.

> The destruction of this country by the enemy exceeds any-thing in history. For many miles every dwelling-house, every Negro cabin, every cotton-gin, every corn-crib, and even chicken-houses have been burned to the ground; every fence torn down and the fields torn up by the hoofs of hors-es and wheels of wagons. Many hundreds of persons are utterly without shelter. But for our prompt attacks Natchitoches would have been burned to the ground, and also the little village of Cloutierville, both of them having been fired in several places.[20]

One of the first Federal targets was the town of Alexandria. Local resident E. R. Biossat stood on Front Street and watched helplessly as the invaders poured in. "Every store in the town was at once forcibly entered and robbed of every article," said Biossat, "and the cases, windows, iron chests, shelves, etc., broken to a thousand fragments." Along with their men, blue-clad officers took part in the plundering. "Private houses were entered in like manner, and robbed and desecrated," he con-tinued. Biossat's black servant had his silver watch stolen by two Federal privates. Biossat later witnessed two marines accompanied by a navy officer enter the Second Street home of Mrs. Caleb Taylor. They removed the clock from her mantle, wrapped it in one of her quilts, and took it back to their gun-boat. Two other marines and an officer plundered the Episcopal church.[21]

A little boy four years old, the son of a Confederate captain named Kelso, proudly proclaimed before a crowd of Yankees that he was a "rebel." A witness reported what happened next.

> One of them applied a cord to his neck and suspended him as if he intended to inflict death. When gasping for breath he was taken down and asked if he were still a rebel. The stout-hearted little patriot reaffirmed his rebellious sentiments and was again suspended, and so remained until a returning sense of humanity of some of the by-standers compelled his release. The child bore for some days the mark on his neck.[22]

On May 13 the Union army was ordered to abandon Alexandria, and Banks issued his usual perfunctory orders that the town be spared destruction. Fires began breaking out that very morning, even before the commanding general himself had time to mount up and leave. One store on Front Street was torched, and a soldier was seen running about, dousing everything combustible with a turpentine-soaked mop. He was overheard to say they were "preparing the place for Hell!" Assisted by a strong wind, and more turpentine where needed, flames soon engulfed all Alexandria.

A reporter from the *St. Louis Republican* called the suffering there "appalling."

> Women gathered their helpless babes in their arms, rushing frantically through the streets with screams and cries that would have melted the hardest hearts to tears; little boys and girls running hither and thither crying for their mothers and fathers; old men leaning on a staff for support to their trembling limbs, hurrying away from the suffocating heat of their burning dwellings and homes.

White and black, free and slave, rich and poor, and those of all political persuasions saw the fire consume everything they owned. Two prominent Alexandria Unionists, John K. Elgee and J. Madison Wells, lost fine and richly furnished homes and their possessions to the flames.[23]

Even after the Federal withdrawal, Louisianians in this region continued to suffer at the hands of Unionist jayhawkers. Gangs of these marauders carried on what one historian called a "regime of rape, murder, and pillage," until suppressed by Confederate troops and home guard units.[24]

Chapter 13

"No Strict Dichotomy"

The Lieber Code

At the midpoint of the war, Washington issued a new list of rules—General Order Number 100—it was claimed would henceforth govern the conduct of Federal troops. Prior to this declaration, the Articles of War (passed by the Ninth Congress in 1806) set forth "the rules and articles by which the armies of the United States shall be governed." Precursor to the Uniform Code of Military Justice, the Articles remained in effect throughout the war period, 1861-65. Among other things, an officer was required to "keep good order, and to the utmost of his power, redress all abuses or disorders, which may be committed by any officer or soldier under his command." The statute prescribed punishment for those who "commit waste or spoil" or who "maliciously destroy any property whatsoever, belonging to the inhabitants of the United States."[1] Denying the legality of secession, Federals were of course left with no choice but to define Southerners as "inhabitants of the United States." The Provisional Congress of the Confederate States, setting up their own military establishment in 1861, adopted the 1806 act word for word, only substituting "Confederate" in place of "United" States.[2]

General Order Number 100 originated with Francis Lieber. Born in Berlin, Lieber (1800-72) immigrated to Boston in 1827, by then already a veteran of Gebhard von Blücher's army and a graduate of the University of Jena. He soon made an impression as editor of the *Encyclopedia Americana* but did his most important work during a long tenure as professor of history and political economy at South Carolina College. Lieber's *Manual of Political Ethics* and *On Civil Liberty and Self-Government* established his reputation for being a firm advocate of strong, centralized government. "I, as a native German who longed for the Unity of his country from his very boyhood cannot be expected to lean much toward State Rights doctrine." In 1857 he accepted a professorship at Columbia College in New York. He soon became a supporter of the new Republican party and its 1860 standard-bearer, Abraham Lincoln.[3]

To his credit, Lieber was from the beginning of the war troubled by Union army excesses. On November 13, 1862, he wrote to Gen. Henry W. Halleck in Washington, suggesting that "a set of rules and definitions" be established. Lieber was himself given the task and within a few months had completed a draft. A board of officers then made revisions, omitting some items "which I regret," wrote Lieber. "Instructions for the Government of Armies of the United States in the Field" was published by the U.S. War Department as General Order Number 100 on April 24, 1863.[4]

Though Lieber was in general pleased with the document that bore his name, he still fretted about crimes being committed against civilians by the United States Army. Only weeks after the code officially went into effect, he wrote again to Halleck.

> I believe it is now time for you to issue a strong order, directing attention to those paragraphs in the Code which prohibit devastations, demolition of private property, etc. I know by letters from the West and the South, written by men on our side, of course, that the wanton destruction of property by our men is alarming. It does incalculable injury. It demoralizes our troops, it annihilates wealth irrevocably and makes a return to a state of peace and peaceful minds more and more difficult.[5]

Halleck was a highly intelligent man who found in Lieber a

congenial correspondent, a mind equal to his own, one he might share his thoughts with on many subjects. Lieber took Halleck at face value, no doubt assuming his new friend possessed an integrity to match his intellect. "Halleck's life demonstrated no strict dichotomy," wrote a biographer, "between success and failure, action and inaction, decision and indecision."[6] Halleck's double-mindedness on the matter of crimes committed by his army evidences a more profound defect: difficulty in differentiating between sincerity and deceit, truth and falsehood, right and wrong.

The armed forces of the United States had of course been committing many of the very acts proscribed by Lieber's Code, and after its adoption those crimes only increased in frequency and ferocity—with Halleck's approval and even encouragement. Ostensibly forbidden were crimes against civilians that would come to define the Federal war effort: "wanton devastation of a district" (Art. 16), "all robbery, all pillage or sacking" (Art. 44), and "arson . . . assaults . . . theft" (Art. 47).

In its 157 articles, exceptions often nullified a rule promulgated. For example, those who administered martial law were admonished to observe "the principles of justice, honor, and humanity" (Art. 4). "To save the country," *however,* "is paramount to all other considerations" (Art. 5). In order that women and children be allowed to evacuate, the enemy should be informed of a commander's intention to bombard a city, *but only if* the element of surprise is thought unnecessary (Art. 19). Noncombatants were not to be "murdered, enslaved, or carried off to distant parts" *when* this did not conflict with "the overruling demands of a vigorous war" (Art. 23).[7]

Confederate secretary of war James A. Seddon denounced this duplicity, characterizing General Order Number 100 as "a confused, unassorted, and undiscriminating compilation." A commander "under this code may pursue a line of conduct in accordance with principles of justice, faith, and honor, or he may justify conduct correspondent with the barbarous hordes who overran the Roman Empire, or who, in the Middle Ages, devastated the continent of Asia and menaced the civilization of Europe."[8]

Maj. Gen. Henry W. Halleck

Clouded by loopholes and lax enforcement, the code still endorsed the concept of "hard war." "Military necessity . . . allows of all destruction of property, and obstruction of the ways and channels of traffic, travel, or communication, and of all withholding of sustenance or means of life from the enemy" (Art. 15). "War is not carried on by arms alone. It is lawful to starve the hostile belligerent, armed or unarmed, so that it leads to the speedier subjugation of the enemy" (Art. 17). If non-combatants are "expelled" from (or attempt to flee?) a place under siege, it is permissible "to drive them back, so as to hasten on the surrender" (Art. 18). War is defined as a struggle between states, not merely between the armed forces of those states. "The citizen or native of a hostile country is thus an enemy, as one of the constituents of the hostile state or nation, and as such is subjected to the hardships of war" (Art. 21).

"The ultimate object of all modern war is a renewed state of peace" was the disingenuous conclusion of the Lieber Code. "The more vigorously wars are pursued, the better it is for humanity" (Art. 29).[9]

And for that we will hate you forever & one day establish an honourable gov't & our own.

Chapter 14

"We Spent the Rest of That Day in the Dungeon"

Women and Children in Prison

When the troops of Brig. Gen. Kenner Garrard entered Roswell, Georgia, on July 6, 1864, they found a factory operating (though not at full capacity), capable of producing 30,000 yards of woolen cloth per month. A cotton mill nearby held 216 looms and could turn out 191,000 yards of cotton cloth monthly, in addition to huge quantities of thread and rope. Another factory stood about a mile and a half outside of town. In all the combined value of the machinery at the three plants was estimated at four hundred thousand dollars, the worth of the businesses perhaps one million dollars. Some four hundred women were employed at the mills, and many children accompanied their mothers to work. Spinners, pressers, and carders made little more than their expenses for board; skilled weavers earned much more; all were glad to have gainful employment. Not surprisingly, the primary customer for textiles produced at the mills was the Confederate government, for use by that country's army.

At least some investors backing the enterprise were British and French. Garrard observed a French tricolor flying over the woolen factory, "but seeing no Federal flag above it I had the building burnt," he reported to Sherman. "All are burnt."[1]

"The women and children filed out of the structure at once," wrote a Federal artilleryman, "and stood in quiet wonder on the banks of the stream, watching our preparations for the

105

destruction of the mills." A Union officer riding through Roswell observed the scene. "About 400 factory girls lined the sides of the road as we passed presenting quite a sad appearance, as they were thrown out of employment and seemed not to know where they would go or what to do."[2]

Sherman knew what to do. Within hours he ordered Garrard to "arrest the owners and employees and send them, under guard, charged with treason, to Marietta." He expected that the "poor women will howl." Children were to accompany them. He was delighted that the mills had been burned, but furious to learn that the manager tried to avert destruction by flying a neutral flag. "Should you," Sherman wrote Garrard, "under the impulse of anger, natural at contemplating such perfidy, hang the wretch, I approve the act before hand."[3]

The prisoners were loaded onto 110 wagons and transported thirteen miles in the July heat over rutted roads to Marietta. First held at the Georgia Military Institute, from Marietta the women and children were sent by rail to Nashville. They finally began arriving in Louisville, Kentucky, about two weeks after their arrest. "Only think of it!" wrote the New York Tribune. "Four hundred weeping and terrified Ellens, Susans, and Maggies transported . . . away from their lovers and brothers of the sunny south, and all for the offense of weaving tent-cloth and spinning stocking yarn!"[4]

Their new residences were a house that had been recently seized on Broadway between Twelfth and Thirteenth Streets and a newly constructed building between Tenth and Eleventh. The Federal prison for men was close by, as was the terminal of the Louisville & Nashville Railroad.[5] A Wisconsin reporter visited the women and came away thoroughly disgusted. "They uttered loud and bitter curses on General Sherman," asking why he drove them from their homes, why he left them nothing, why he arrested women and children and sent them to faraway imprisonment. Rather than consider those rather serious questions, the Wisconsinite spent his entire article making fun of the girls' grammar and accent. The Louisville Daily Journal claimed that the women had begged to leave Georgia; that Sherman's "enlarged and generous spirit of humanity" prompted him to send them to where "they could find work and security." The editor of that paper reported their new rooms "clean and airy," their children "rosy-cheeked."[6]

One inmate, Rose McDonald, described her imprisonment as "a living death." "We slept on the bare floor without a pillow, blanket or bedding of any kind, and were never alone, for day and night an armed guard was with us. . . . After a time I sickened and lay for several days unnoticed on the bare floor, suffering from a scorching fever."[7]

A notice appeared in the *Journal*, a call to Louisville citizens from the Commission for the Aid of Refugees, appealing for funds. "There are children of every age, some so attenuated as to be living skeletons, perishing for want of proper care," it read. Dozens of families crowded together, many were sick, and all needed "proper care and support."[8]

Dr. Mary Edwards Walker was sent by the military authorities to provide that care. She was appointed "Surgeon in Charge" of the Louisville Female Military Prison hospital in late September.[9] "It was during my illness that I first saw the anomalous creature that was put over us for our sins," wrote McDonald. "If ever a fiend in human guise walked this earth it did it in that woman's body." A two-year-old, the child of a prisoner, sat at the top of stairs when Dr. Walker "came storming along," she remembered. "'Get out of my way, you little brat!' she cried, and kicked the little thing down the stairs."

> Some kind ladies of Louisville promised us a Christmas dinner, and every day we talked of it over our scanty means. At last the long wished-for day arrived, but we did by no means spend it as we had hoped, for the Doctor furnished each room with a loaf of bread and a pitcher of water and locked up the inmates for the day. She received the dinner and she alone knew what became of it.
>
> During Christmas morning some Confederate prisoners were marched past our window. . . . I and others waived [*sic*] our handkerchiefs to them. The Doctor saw us, consequently we spent the rest of that day in the dungeon.

When an army inspector came, inmates complained about

Dr. Walker and presented a statement of their grievances. There was no change, except that Walker found out about the protest. "She was like an insane person after that," said McDonald.[10]

It became increasingly difficult to justify the incarceration of hundreds of women whose only crime had been that they worked for a living. Over a period of months, as the war wound down and Confederate armies surrendered, the women and children were released in small groups to find their way home.

Chapter 15

"Make It a Desolation"

The Shelling of Atlanta

"Let us destroy Atlanta and make it a desolation," said Sherman as Union shells rained down on that city. "One thing is certain, whether we get inside Atlanta or not, it will be a used up community by the time we are done with it."[1]

After a two-month campaign through northern Georgia, by mid-July the Union army was camped outside Atlanta. Over the next three weeks Sherman's field artillery fired on the city. "A battery of twenty pieces is posted near my headquarters and is booming away night and day into Atlanta," one Federal officer wrote home. "In the night it is particularly noisy and rest-breaking."[2] Superintendent of the Atlanta gas works, Mr. Warner, was himself attempting to rest at eleven o'clock on the night of August 3 when one of those iron projectiles crashed into his home at the corner of Elliott and Rhodes Streets. Both his legs were severed by the missile and he died within two hours. Warner's six-year-old daughter was cut in two by the same shot. Elsewhere that day a man, his wife, and their daughter were killed by shell fragments. An unidentified woman died when shrapnel shattered the window of a train arriving from Macon. One lady, a refugee from Rome, was ironing clothes when a shell hit her directly, tearing her to pieces. Citizens soon began to dig pits and "bomb proofs" in their yards, and sandbags went up around some buildings. "I do not think there is a house in the city but what has had a shell or shot to fall or pass very near it," wrote a Southern newsman.[3] Little did he know that Atlanta's ordeal was only beginning.

Sherman ordered heavy artillery be sent by rail from Chattanooga, "with which we can pick out almost any house in the town," he boasted. "Let me know if the 4½-inch guns have come and where you will place them," he wrote Maj. Gen. George H. Thomas on August 8. "I would like to have them at work to-morrow."[4] Every Union gun within range of the city— 223 cannon of all size—opened fire on August 9. As many as five thousand rounds of shot and shell fell on Atlanta that one day, the heaviest bombardment ever inflicted on an American city. It went on day and night for another three weeks. Six members of one family were killed by a direct hit on their shelter.[5] A forty-two-pound shell crashed through the roof of the Presbyterian church on Marietta Street, penetrated the floor, and exploded in a basement Sunday School room crowded with those seeking shelter. Miraculously no one was killed, though a man lost his right arm.[6] Another shell hit the sidewalk on Alabama Street, mortally wounding black barber Solomon Luckie as he stood outside his shop.[7] One lady was killed instantly by an explosion on the street in front of the Express Office.[8] There seemed no end to the carnage. During the shelling, one surgeon reported having performed 107 amputations on men, women, and children.

With thousands of shells and solid shot falling on the city every day, citizens tried to discern warning signs. Incoming shells with burning fuses might be observed as they fell—"like meteors or shooting stars"—but those with percussion caps gave only a brief whistle before suddenly exploding on impact.[9] Fires were sometimes started by the explosions, and incendiary shot were thrown into the city to ignite wooden structures. "We could see the thick volumes of smoke and then the lurid flames shooting along the horizon," wrote a reporter for the *New York Herald.* "We could also hear the fire bells ringing. Some of our batteries are pouring red hot shot on the town." Atlanta's volunteer firefighters braved the shelling to battle flames, well aware that Federal gunners would increase their rate of fire any time they observed the glow from a new conflagration.[10]

Most Confederate troops were engaged in parrying Federal advances or manning the trenches outside Atlanta during the bombardment. Of course, Southern soldiers might be found on the streets of the city they were defending as they redeployed, transported supplies, or perhaps were taken to a hospital. But enemy troops were not the target of Sherman's indiscriminate shelling of Atlanta's homes, businesses, and churches. Clearly, terror was his objective.

An Indiana doctor serving in Sherman's army toured Atlanta after its evacuation.

> I had often heard of the terrors of a bombardment of a crowded city but I never realized it before. Houses were shattered and torn in every shape that can be imagined, some utterly destroyed and some but little injured. Some had shell through the doors, some places the shell had burst inside of a house and torn it all to pieces. . . .
>
> I would not for a great deal have missed that ride through Atlanta [concluded the Hoosier]. It almost paid me for the whole campaign.[11]

"You defended Atlanta on a line so close to town that every cannon-shot . . . that overshot their mark, went into the habitations of women and children," wrote Sherman to Gen. John Bell Hood only weeks later,[12] blaming the Confederate commander for his own deliberate shelling of civilians.

Chapter 16

"As Captors, We Have a Right to It"

The Forced Evacuation
of Atlanta

As soon as Sherman occupied Atlanta in September 1864 he, in his own words, "at once set about a measure already ordered, of which I had thought much and long, viz., to remove the entire civil population, and to deny to all civilians from the rear the expected profits of civil trade. Hundreds of sutlers and traders were waiting at Nashville and Chattanooga, greedy to reach Atlanta with their wares and goods, with which to drive a profitable trade with the inhabitants."[1]

Sherman had long distrusted entrepreneurs who followed his army—especially when they happened to be Jews. In July 1862 he stopped all cotton trading in Memphis carried on by "Jews and speculators." He was not alone in his bigotry. While Sherman complained of what he called "swarms of Jews,"[2] Maj. Gen. Ulysses S. Grant issued orders banning "speculators coming South," adding that "Jews should receive special attention." In December, Grant went even further, expelling "Jews, as a class," from his Department of the Tennessee.[3]

But Sherman had additional motives for depopulating Atlanta. With no civilians left, the place would be easier for him to fortify. More importantly, he did not want the responsibility of caring for "a poor population" while "listening to [their] everlasting complaints and special grievances." In his view, Atlanta no longer belonged to those who lived there. "As captors, we have a right to it." And forcing the residents of Atlanta from their city would send a message to other Confederates fighting for their homes. "I knew that the people of the South would read in this measure two important conclusions," said the general, "one, that, we were in earnest; and the other, if they were sincere in their common and popular clamor 'to die in the last ditch' that the opportunity would soon come."[4]

On September 7, Sherman sent a letter to Gen. John Bell Hood, commander of the Confederate Army of Tennessee. "I have deemed it to the interest of the United States that the citizens now residing in Atlanta should remove, those who prefer it to go south, and the rest north." A truce was proposed, during which those civilians forced to refugee south would be transported to the care of Confederates at the village of Rough and Ready in Clayton County. "I do not consider that I have any alternative in this matter," Hood responded, agreeing to the terms, though, "In the name of God and humanity, I protest."

Sherman exploded in anger. In another letter to Hood he accused Southerners of starting the war, seizing forts, and making prisoners of "the very garrisons sent to protect your people against Negroes and Indians." Hood took up the challenge, replying in a long letter to Sherman that countered each of his arguments, holding that Southern "masters, slaves, and Indians . . . with a unanimity unexampled in the history of the world, [are] warring against your attempts to become their masters."

When Atlanta's mayor asked Sherman to reconsider his plan in light of the suffering forced evacuation would cause, the general was adamant. His order was "not designed to meet the humanities of the case," but to further military goals. "War is cruelty, and you cannot refine it. . . . you cannot have peace and a division of our country. . . . The United States does and must assert its authority, wherever it once had power; for, if it relaxes one bit to pressure, it is gone." Sherman's superiors in Washington agreed with his action. "The course which you have pursued in removing rebel families from Atlanta," wrote chief of staff Henry Halleck, "is fully approved by the War Department."[5]

Many Atlanta families had already fled the city, a few now opted to go north, and some managed to stay despite the order. A total of 1,644 adults, children, and servants officially registered to board Union railroad cars for the journey south to Rough and Ready, though the actual number involved was probably greater.[6]

The Braumuller family was one of those that decided to head north, to Nashville, in search of family. Mrs. Braumuller's son described their departure from Atlanta, which took place under the supervision of Union troops. "Each family could have a fourth of a box car, they said. Freight cars were very small, not much larger than a wagon. Mother decided that she would try to save two pianos we had in the house, for these would be easier to convert into ready cash." She begged that she might have a whole car to move the pianos, admitting there was no use trying to save any of her other possessions. "The officers took the hint and provided the car, sending men to help move the bulky music boxes. By letting her go with them, the men could help themselves to the other valuables without any questions being asked."

Another witness, Mary Gay, saw wagonloads of expensive furniture stolen by Federals being transferred to rail cars for shipment north.[7]

Atlantans fleeing south were also victimized. Crowds waiting for cars were told that theirs would be the last train out of Atlanta, but for a sufficient price a place might yet be found for them. Some paid as much as two hundred dollars—perhaps all they had—for their "free" ticket. Another ruse was to allow only part of a family to board before demanding the bribe, since everyone feared separation from loved ones. One Federal officer, identified only as "Captain S.," assured those departing that he would protect property left behind—only to sell it as soon as the train pulled out. This captain promised one woman that he would move into her empty house to keep an eye on its contents. The stolen furniture was quickly on a train headed north.

A reporter from the *New York Times* was saddened by the sight of those waiting at the train depot, exiles who "cast many a long lingering look at their once happy home, which they were now about to abandon, perhaps forever."[8]

Northern soldiers were approached by women trying to barter vegetables and even wild grapes they had gathered. "They will not take money but want bread or flour or meat," wrote an Indiana doctor. "They say that money would be worthless to them as there is no place that they would be able to buy anything with it. They tell some pitiful stories of starving children, and the worst is that they are true."[9]

One refugee saw "aged grandmothers upon the verge of the grave, tender girls in the first bloom of young womanhood, and little babes not three days old in the arms of sick mothers," all homeless now and "thrown out upon the cold charity of the world."[10]

Sherman commandeered a house on Court House Square for his headquarters. With Atlanta now largely rid of its homeowners, other officers took what houses they wanted. Enlisted men had to content themselves with dismantling buildings and using the lumber to build shelters in squares and public parks. "The African Methodist Episcopal Church, built by the colored people with their hard earnings, was also demolished by our soldiers," reported a Northerner. The army's horses roamed city cemeteries.[11]

Chapter 17

"Plundering Dreadfully from All Accounts"

Hunter in the Shenandoah

Maj. Gen. David Hunter, though a West Point graduate and professional soldier, demonstrated little ability as a Union military commander during the first two years of war. In late spring 1864 he launched a raid on Virginia's agriculturally productive Shenandoah Valley that proved beyond a doubt he was more than competent when combating unarmed civilians.

On May 24, at the beginning of the operation, near Newtown a Federal wagon train loaded with supplies was captured by Confederate guerrillas under the command of Maj. Harry Gilmor,[1] and at least one U.S. Army sergeant was wounded. Hunter was furious, ordering the torching of houses in the neighborhood where his loss had occurred. "In case a train or a man is fired on by anyone behind our lines," wrote a member of his staff, "houses of Secessionists and their property are to be burned without mercy." One of the homes torched belonged to Rev. J. Wolff, admitted by the staff officer to be "a worthy, upright man." Another residence was rented by a Mrs. Wilson. Charged with "feeding and harboring" Confederates, she was arrested and her possessions were destroyed. Other homes along the route of the advancing army were burned if they were the suspected meeting places for Confederate guerrillas or near locations Federals had suffered casualties at their hands.[2]

Hunter also ordered that "secession sympathizers" within a radius of ten miles from where army supplies were lost be made to pay "five times the value of such property." His troops were ordered to "seize and hold in close military custody the persons assessed until such payment shall have been made."[3]

It was dangerous, too, for civilians to give inaccurate information to their enemy, as reported by one on Hunter's staff. "The General asked me to go into Woodstock to ascertain who the parties were that attempted to confuse our scouts yesterday as he wished to burn a few houses."[4]

At Harrisonburg, the newspaper was immediately targeted by the invaders. "The office of the *Rockingham Register* was gutted," reported the same officer, "the press broken up, and the debris burned in the street, the rain falling on the heap of ashes."[5]

Confederate lieutenant colonel John S. Mosby had his own way of dealing with U.S. Army house burners who could be individually and positively identified. One such arsonist was led to the ruins of the home he was responsible for torching and there executed. "Shot for house-burning," read the placard placed on his back. "Mosby, then dispatched a letter to the Federal commander in the Valley," remembered one of his partisans, "which contained an account of this transaction, and a declaration that he would continue to have all house-burners executed who might fall into his hands."[6] It did no good.

Hunter's soldiers entered Staunton on Monday, June 6, and "are plundering dreadfully from all accounts," wrote an officer.[7] The town would be occupied by Federals then liberated by Confederates twice over the next four days. While in possession of Staunton, Yankees burned the carriage factory, shoe factory, and stables; plundered stores; and pillaged homes. They invaded the office and smashed the press of the *Vindicator*. Staunton's other newspaper, the *Spectator*, suffered a similar fate, its type being scattered on the street. The city's firefighting equipment was destroyed. Estimates for damage done within the city limits would run as high as one million dollars.

Mayor N. K. Trout was arrested, as was city councilman B. F. Points—the latter jailed for expressing amusement at Hunter's precipitous retreat the day before. George W. Fuller was accused of being a "spy" because he delivered letters to Southern soldiers.[8] The troops of "Hen-roost Hunter," wrote the editor of the *Vindicator* a month later, "robbed the man of means and widow with her mite of whatever their larder contained. . . . Some two or three who had been suspected of sympathizing with the enemy and who, report says, claimed protection on this account, suffered as did others, their unionism not being able 'to save their bacon.'"[9]

Mills at Mt. Meridian, Greenville, and Fairfield were burned by Hunter's army.[10] On June 11 began a two-day occupation of Lexington, characterized by one historian as "an orgy of destruction." Soldiers charged into homes looking for valuables and vandalized what they did not take. "Some persons were left destitute and almost starving," wrote one victim. Another resident remembered "dresses torn to pieces in mere wantonness: even the Negro girls had lost their finery." The barracks and classrooms of Virginia Military Institute were looted, then the entire campus was torched. Homes, including that of former governor John Letcher, were set on fire.[11] Letcher's was singled out, according to Hunter, since the owner was guilty of "inciting the population" to resist invasion.[12] Yankees sacked Washington College, "pelting the statue of the father of their country," wrote an officer, "supposing it to represent Jefferson Davis." Viewing the progress of destruction from a nearby hill, that officer declared it "grand," noting that Hunter, too, "seemed to enjoy this scene."[13]

The Stars and Stripes was raised in the town of Liberty on June 16, and immediately plundering of residences and private property broke out. Wherever the blue-clad troops went, civilians were robbed. As an officer conversed with ladies at one home, "soldiers got into the house and commenced to plunder their trunks and bureaus." At another rural residence, the same officer asked directions of a professed Unionist but found troops already busy stealing all that he owned. Soldiers had broken into the loyalist's beehives and were "devouring great chunks of honey with brutal greediness. The honey as they ate it was streaming down their clothes and clotting in their beards."[14]

By the end of June, wrote an historian, "Hunter was applying the torch without restraint or rule."[15] One civilian, a man named Leftwich, reported hearing of Union army defeats.

"This irritated the General so much," wrote an officer, "that he had Leftwich arrested and ordered his house to be burnt. It was a very pretty country residence, and the man had a sweet daughter about sixteen and a nice family."[16] The general's artillery commander came to conclude that Hunter's "mentality was largely dominated by prejudices and antipathies so intense and so violent as to render him at times quite incapable of taking a fair and unbiased view of many military and political situations."[17]

The following month, after Hunter was finally expelled from the Shenandoah Valley of Virginia, Confederate lieutenant general Jubal A. Early marched his army northward into Maryland and Pennsylvania—even for a time threatening Washington, D.C. Early was careful to remind his men "that they are engaged in no marauding expedition, and are not making war upon the defenseless and unresisting."[18] But the Virginian took it upon himself to demand compensation for Hunter's house burning in the Shenandoah. Hagerstown, Maryland, was required to pay twenty thousand dollars. On July 24, Early demanded one hundred thousand dollars from Chambersburg, Pennsylvania, threatening the town's destruction if the money was not forthcoming. "The policy pursued by our army on former occasions had been so lenient, that they did not suppose the threat was in earnest this time," said Early; but when payment was denied, he ordered Chambersburg burned. Col. William Peters, commanding the Twenty-first Virginia Cavalry Regiment, refused to obey. Other Confederate officers actually ordered their men to disobey. Still, the deed was done. "For this act, I, alone, am responsible," confessed the general.

Though Early believed retaliation might put a stop to Federal depredations,[19] he would soon be disappointed. Hunter was no aberration. In coming months the Union war on Southern civilians only intensified. As the editor of the *Staunton Vindicator* pointed out, Yankee behavior demonstrated during Hunter's raid "has served simply to prove conclusively to us that we were not wrong in the estimate we placed upon them many years ago."[20]

Chapter 18

"Nothing Left for Man or Beast"

Sheridan's Devastation

"In the recent temporary occupation of the Valley of Virginia," observed the editor of the *Staunton Vindicator* in the aftermath of Sheridan's raid, "the enemy again exhibited that malignant malice which characterized the invasion of Hunter."[1]

Maj. Gen. Philip Sheridan had replaced David Hunter as Federal commander in August, and Ulysses S. Grant expected greater results. "In pushing up the Shenandoah Valley . . . it is desirable that nothing should be left to invite the enemy to return. Take all provisions, forage, and stock wanted for the use of your command; such as cannot be consumed, destroy."[2] Grant fired off a reminder a few weeks later. "If the war is to last another year, we want the Shenandoah Valley to remain a barren waste."[3] Victory at the Battle of Third Winchester on September 19, 1864, against badly outnumbered Confederates, gave Sheridan opportunity to achieve that objective. What followed came to be known by his victims simply as "The Burning."[4]

First there would be executions. Five of Lt. Col. John S. Mosby's Confederate Rangers were captured and put to death on September 23 to avenge the loss in combat of a Yankee officer. Also taken prisoner by Federals was civilian teenager Henry Rhodes from Front Royal who had hoped to join the partisans.[5] "Rhodes was lashed with ropes between two horses,"

Maj. Gen. Philip H. Sheridan

recounted a friend who witnessed his death, "and dragged in plain sight of his agonized relatives to the open field of our town, where one man volunteered to do the killing, and ordered the helpless, dazed prisoner to stand up in front of him, while he emptied his pistol upon him."[6]

Sheridan's Shenandoah Valley Campaign got underway days later.

[Brig. Gen. George] Custer was to take the west and [Brig. Gen. Wesley] Merritt the east side and burn all barns, mills, haystacks, etc., within a certain area [remembered a Michigan colonel]. Merritt was provoked. He pointed to the west and one could have made a chart of Custer's trail by the columns of black smoke which marked it. The general was manifestly fretting lest Custer should appear to outdo him in zeal in obeying orders, and blamed me as his responsible subordinate, for the delay.

There was no cause for concern, as flames were soon breaking out within Merritt's area of responsibility as well. Women and children begged to have a little flour before his troops burned the mill in Port Republic "on which their very existence seemed to depend." Tears and pleading were in vain.[7] From there Merritt's horsemen rode in the direction of Staunton to continue "burning forage, mills, and such other property as might be serviceable to the rebel army or Confederacy," in Sheridan's words.[8] "The work of incineration was continued," wrote the Michigan colonel, "and clouds of smoke marked the passage of the federal army."[9]

One Vermont soldier claimed to witness no houses set on fire, but "barns, mills, and stacks of hay and grain . . . everything combustible that could aid the enemy during the coming winter was burned, and all cattle and sheep were driven away." That Vermonter and his comrades came upon a country store and a schoolhouse standing nearby. Soon both "suffered the same fate, though in a different way, the material of one being used to cook the contents of the other."[10]

An Ohio surgeon confessed that Union troops were in fact torching residences. "We are burning and destroying everything in this valley, such as wheat stacks, hay stacks, barns, hous-es," he reported in a letter home. "Indeed, there will be noth-ing but heaps of ashes and ruins generally. . . . Thousands of Refugees are fleeing north daily, as nothing but starvation would stare them in the face to stay in this valley the coming winter."[11]

Many of those refugees were pacifists—members of reli-gious sects such as Mennonites and Dunkers—who had for years tried to live above even the conflict of politics. Mennonite D. H. Landis, resettled in Ohio, wrote that the invaders destroyed Shenandoah Valley churches. "The Union army came up the Valley sweeping everything before them like a wild hurricane," said another, "there was nothing left for man or beast." Michael Shank fled to Pennsylvania and there described his experience with Sheridan's "prowlers," men who "commenced pilfering, robbing and plundering."

> [S]quads of them would go to citizens [sic] houses in almost frantic appearance, their faces speaking terror to the inhab-itants, while they were searching every room from cellar to garret, breaking open bureau drawers, chests and closets taking whatever suited their fancy, such as money, watches, jewelry, wearing apparel, etc., at the same time threatening to shoot the inmates of the house if they followed after them. In the meantime our horses, cows and cattle were taken, the grain house was broken open and robbed of its contents and when the body of the army passed up thousands upon thou-sands passed over my farm in a number of columns through corn and cornfields; thus they continued their work of destruction. . . . For several days before we left we saw great columns of smoke rising like dark clouds almost from one mountain to the other.[12]

Other Mennonites lost their homes—as well as barns, live-stock, grain, and all they owned—when Sheridan demanded vengeance for the death of a favorite member of his staff. On October 3, Lt. John Meigs and two other Union soldiers came upon three Virginia cavalrymen, and in the skirmish that fol-lowed one Federal was captured and Meigs was killed. The escaping Federal was confused by the raincoats Confederates had been wearing, giving rise to the tale that they were "bush-whackers." Sheridan branded it "murder" and vowed to avenge the "foul deed" by torching everything within a radius of five miles.[13] "Splendid mansions in great number, in the vicinity, were laid in ashes," remembered a New Yorker.[14] At least twenty houses went up in flames, many those of unoffending Mennonites. Most neighboring families spent the night outside, said a witness, the morning "marked by a dense blanket of smoke and fog that had settled over the country as [if] it were to hide from view the awful effect of the great holocaust of fire of the evening before."[15]

A cavalryman from the Old Dominion described the scene he witnessed.

> On every side, from mountain to mountain, the flames from all the barns, mills, grain and hay stacks, and in very many instances from dwellings, too, were blazing skyward, leaving a smoky train of desolation to mark the footsteps of the devil's inspector-general, and show in a fiery record, that will last as long as the war is remembered, that the United States, under the government of Satan and Lincoln, sent Phil. Sheridan to campaign in the Valley of Virginia.[16]

Sheridan's incendiaries were characterized by one of Mosby's men as "demons of conflagration, rejoicing in the mischief they had wrought."[17] The colonel's policy was to ruthlessly punish those who burned houses, if the guilty could be identified. When Rangers came upon the burning home of a citizen named Province McCormick, they were shown the direction the perpetrators had gone. The nearby Sowers' residence they found in flames, ladies and children in the yard under a downpour of rain. Again the Confederates galloped off in pursuit of the arsonists and soon found them—about ninety in number—torching the home of the Morgan family. Battle ensued, but the Yankees quickly broke and ran. Twenty-nine Federal prisoners were taken, including wounded. Having been caught in the act of house burning, all were put to death on the spot.[18]

"I have destroyed over 2,000 barns, filled with wheat, hay,

and farming implements," Sheridan reported to Grant, along with "over 70 mills, filled with flour and wheat." That told but part of the story, of course, and only hinted at the suffering of civilians, but Sheridan was proud to point out his punishing of noncombatants for the death of Meigs.[19] And he had done it all in less than two weeks.

Unable to vanquish Robert E. Lee on the battlefield, Grant "has turned his arms against the women and children of our land," concluded the longsuffering editor of Staunton's newspaper. "Retribution will come."[20]

Chapter 19

"General Sherman Is Kind of Careless with Fire"

The Burning of Atlanta

"They came burning Atlanta today," wrote ten-year-old Carrie Berry in her diary. "We all dread it because they say that they will burn the last house before they stop."[1]

William Tecumseh Sherman fought long and hard to conquer that city, but now in preparation for his March to the Sea, he determined to leave nothing for Confederates to recover. All railroad property, warehouses, mills, and factories in Atlanta would be leveled.[2] On Friday morning, November 11, 1864, he ordered engineer Orlando M. Poe to "commence the work of destruction at once, but don't use fire until the last moment." Demolition teams had for a week been undermining masonry walls, weakening chimneys, and burying explosive charges. A battering ram of railroad iron was required to shatter the stone walls of the railroad depot. That night flames broke out in several parts of the city, destroying more than twenty residences, "the works of some of the soldiers," according to witness David Conyngham, "who expected to get some booty under cover of the fires." Atlanta's fire engines were being loaded aboard freight cars, bound for Chattanooga, but went into action by order of Maj. Gen. Henry W. Slocum. "Though Slocum knew that the city was doomed," continued Conyngham, "according to his just notions of things it should be done officially. No officer or soldier had a right to fire it without orders."

Those orders came three days later, as the Federal army marched out of the city. "All is solemnly desolate," noted Ohio captain George W. Pepper, commenting on the damage done to Atlanta by Federal shelling three months earlier. "Clouds of smoke, as we passed through, were bursting from several princely mansions. Every house of importance was burned on Whitehall street." Other buildings, public and private, were consumed. "This is the penalty of rebellion," concluded Pepper.[3]

"I rode through the city while the fire was at its height," said artillery officer Thomas Osborn. "All the storehouses, manu-factories, railroad buildings and such large blocks as might readily be converted into storehouses were burned." Though Osborn saw no residences deliberately fired, he conceded that advancing flames claimed nearby homes and "the center of the city was pretty thoroughly burned out."[4]

That night an army band played "John Brown's Body" as the troops continued their trek south. Col. Adin Underwood of Massachusetts was awestruck by the scene.

> No darkness—in place of it a great glare of light from acres of burning buildings. This strange light, and the roaring of the flames that licked up everything habitable, the intermittent explosions of powder, stored ammo. and projectiles, streams of fire that shot up here and there from heaps of cotton bales and oil factories, the crash of falling buildings, and the change, as if by a turn of the kaleidoscope, of strong walls and proud structures into heaps of desolation; all this made a dreadful picture of the havoc of war, and of its unrelenting horrors.

By seven o'clock the next morning Sherman's engineers estimated that 37 percent of the city had already burned, and the fire continued to spread. Several churches escaped, though most did not. Atlanta's first house of worship built for blacks, on Jenkins Street, went up in flames. The Medical College was spared when Dr. Peter D'Alvigny confronted soldiers igniting straw and broken furniture they had piled in the entrance hall. The doctor shouted that sick and wounded soldiers were still inside, throwing open the door to prove it.[5]

On the evening of that second day Maj. Ward Nichols of Sherman's staff described what he saw:

> The heaven is one expanse of lurid fire; the air is filled with flying, burning cinders; buildings covering two hundred acres are in ruins or in flames; every instant there is the sharp detonation or the smothered booming sound of exploding shells and powder concealed in the buildings, and then the sparks and flame shoot away up into the black red roof, scattering cinders far and wide.[6]

An Ohio infantryman witnessed "an ocean of fire" sweeping over Atlanta, "leaving nothing but the smoldering ruins of this once beautiful city."[7]

As darkness fell on the fire's second day, James Patten, surgeon with the Federal army, paused on a rural road south of the city. "We could see Atlanta burning," wrote the doctor. "I looked at my watch and could see the time very plainly at a distance of ten miles."[8]

The *Daily Intelligencer* later made a detailed street-by-street report on the results of the fire, concluding that two-thirds of Atlanta lay in ashes, with much of the rest damaged by

Atlanta in ruins

Sherman's earlier shelling. "The stillness of the grave for weeks reigned over this once bustling, noisy city."[9]

Major Nichols was told that the holocaust devoured no fewer than five thousand buildings before burning itself out. "General Sherman is kind of careless with fire," observed the major.[10]

Chapter 20

"They Took Everything That Was Not Red-Hot or Nailed Down"

March to the Sea

"Can we whip the South?" wrote William T. Sherman to Henry W. Halleck in 1863. "If we can, our numerical majority has both the natural and constitutional right to govern. If we cannot whip them, they contend for the natural right to select their own government." To keep that from happening—to insure that Southerners *not* have the right to select their own government—"we will remove and destroy every obstacle—if need be, take every life, every acre of land, every particle of property, everything that to us seems proper."[1] A year later, on the eve of his march through Georgia, Sherman boasted, "I am going into the very bowels of the Confederacy, and propose to leave a trail that will be recognized fifty years hence." It would be, he assured Halleck, "a track of desolation."[2]

Even before launching his March to the Sea, Sherman had begun making his mark on the people of Georgia. "We are drawing full rations, besides preying off the country," wrote a Union officer from Summerville, Georgia, in October.[3] Another remarked that same month how raiding parties returned with all manner of food taken from civilians. "The men lived high off the country and brought back lots of plunder."[4] Ike Derricotte, a black man living in Athens, remembered that "Yankees just went around takin' whatever they wanted . . . and laughed about it like they hadn't been stealin'."[5] Though troops were officially prohibited from robbing civilians, officers almost always turned a blind eye when it happened. The men in the ranks well knew what "Uncle Billy" expected of them.

Troops marched out of burning Atlanta, heading to Covington by way of Lithonia and Stone Mountain.[6] When they left Covington for Macon, wrote local resident Dolly Lunt Burge,

> They robbed every house on their road of provisions, sometimes taking every piece of meat, blankets, & wearing apparel, silver & arms of every description. They would take silk dresses and put them under their saddles & things for which they had no use. Is this the way to make us love them & their union? Let the poor people answer whom they have deprived of every mouthful of meat & of their stock to make any. Our mills, too, they have burned, destroying an immense amount of property.[7]

In Madison the railroad depot, tracks, cotton, and public property quickly went up in flames. Businesses were plundered, but of course soldiers were unable to transport much property with them. Instead, they destroyed all they could and amused themselves by such pranks as wearing women's hats taken from milliners' shops. Troops entered homes to continue their work of vandalism. Anything portable—china, silverware, small items of furniture—was thrown from windows. Pianos and wall mirrors were simply smashed where they were.[8]

In Henry County, southeast of Atlanta, when soldiers came to the plantation home of Jim Smith they were not content merely to steal and destroy. A former slave, Charlie Tye Smith, recalled how "Ole Marse Jim" was made to

> pull off his boots and run bare-footed through a cane brake with half a bushel of potatoes tied around his neck; then they made him put his boots back on and carried him down to the mill and tied him to the water post. They were getting ready to break his neck when one of Master's slaves, "Ole Peter Smith," asked them if they intended to kill Marse Jim, and when they said "Yes," Peter choked up and said, "Well, please, suh, let me die with old Marse!"

With that, the Yankees ended their fun and left.[9]

At the Monroe County plantation of Cal Robinson, the invaders "ransacked the place, took all the victuals from the white folks and give 'em to the slaves," remembered one little girl. After the soldiers left the food was returned "'cause they was our own white folks and they always done give us plenty of everything."[10] That was the experience, too, of Emma Hurley, a slave who lived in Lexington. After stealing anything they found of value, Yankees threw meat from the smokehouse to the slaves, but after they left, most was returned. "The Yankees poured out all the syrup and destroyed everything they could," remembered Emma.[11] "They took everything that was not red-hot or nailed down," said Marshal Butler, a slave in Wilkes County.[12]

At the Glenn plantation south of Lexington, soldiers harassed Mrs. Glenn, pulling and jerking her long hair, trying to make her tell them where valuables might be hidden. The Yankees invited slaves to help themselves to meat from the smokehouse. Black children were crying and upset, remembered former slave Martha Colquitt,

> because we loved Mistress and didn't want nobody to bother her. They made out like they were goin' to kill her if she didn't tell 'em what they wanted to know, but after a while they let her alone. . . . After the Yankees was done gone off Grandma began to fuss, "Now, them soldiers was tellin' us what ain't so, 'cause ain't nobody got no right to take what belongs to Master and Mistress."[13]

At the nearby Echols plantation troops invited slaves to take all they wanted from the smokehouse as well as personal property from the master's home and then go where they wanted. Former slave Robert Shepherd recounted that none took them up on their offer of appropriating what was not theirs. When the invaders had gone, Mr. Echols called all of his bondsmen together. He was overcome with emotion and could barely speak, recalled Robert. "Master said he never knowed before how good we loved him. He told us he had done tried to be good to us and had done the best he could for us and that he was mighty proud of the way every one of us had done behaved ourselves."[14]

"Madam, I have orders to burn this house," said one Federal to a resident on the road from Madison to Milledgeville. She replied that she hoped they would not burn the home of defenseless women.

"I'll insure it for fifty dollars," he replied.

"I've got no fifty dollars to pay for insuring it; and if it depends upon that, it must burn."

An offer to "insure" property was one way Federals found to extort cash from their victims. "Soon as he saw he couldn't frighten me into giving him anything, he went to plundering," she said.[15]

Louise Caroline Cornwell watched as troops took "every living thing on the farm—took every bushel of corn and fodder, oats and wheat—every bee gum." They then put the torch to the gin house, blacksmith shop, and stored cotton. "Gen. [Oliver O.] Howard and staff officers came at tea time," remembered Mrs. Cornwell. Howard was known for his supposed piety. "We managed to have something to eat for that meal, which was the last for several days, and while Gen. Howard sat at the table and asked God's blessings, the sky was red from flames of burning houses."[16]

Kate Latimer Nichols, twenty-seven, was sick and bedridden when the Yankees arrived at her farm home near Milledgeville. Two soldiers forced their way past a servant who guarded the door to her room and raped her. "Poor woman," wrote a neighbor in her diary, "I fear that she has been driven crazy." Indeed, the victim never recovered from the ordeal, dying in a mental institution.[17]

At Milledgeville, Georgia's capital until shortly after the Civil War, soldiers wrecked the library and destroyed priceless artifacts housed in the museum there. A bridge leading to the town had been burned to slow the advance of the Federal army, and when Sherman learned of this he ordered that some nearby house be randomly chosen for destruction.

At Sandersville, Confederates destroyed a supply of fodder before retreating. On Sherman's orders several houses in the neighborhood were torched in retaliation as his men ransacked the town. "In war," said Sherman when questioned about it, "everything is right which prevents anything. If bridges are burned, I have a right to burn all houses near it." This was in accordance with his orders, issued back on November 9. He then made it clear that "should guerillas or bushwhackers molest our march, or should the inhabitants burn bridges, obstruct roads, or other wise manifest local hostility, then army commanders should order and enforce a devastation more or less relentless."[18]

Maj. James Austin Connolly agreed wholeheartedly with his commander. Any civilians who would dare destroy food or fodder before Federals could confiscate it for their own use would be severely punished.

> Let them do it if they dare. We'll burn every house, barn, church, and everything else we come to; we'll leave their families houseless and without food; their towns will *all* be destroyed, and nothing but the most complete desolation will be found in our track. This army will not be trifled with. If citizens raise their hands against us to retard our march or play the guerrilla against us, neither youth nor age nor sex will be respected. Everything must be destroyed. . . . We have gone so far now in our triumphal march that we will not be balked.[19]

"We have Sherman's word that it is his wish to conduct the war on civilized principles," mocked Henry Timrod, assistant editor of the *Columbia Daily South Carolinian.*

> The inhabitants of an invaded district have no right to annoy an invading army in any way. To plant a single obstacle in the path of the beneficent power which comes to take care of their property and to relieve them of the "weight of too much liberty," is a crime justly provocative of the bitterest retaliation. . . . This is the Yankee version of the laws of civilized war. It is a piece with Sherman's mode of thinking and writing on every subject.[20]

Mrs. Nora Canning and her elderly husband certainly offered no resistance when Federal troops arrived at their home near Louisville. The soldiers insisted that Mr. Canning show them where a quantity of syrup had been hidden in the swamp. The old gentleman told them he was unable to walk that far, so they brought a mule for him to ride. While he was gone troops fired the gin house, granary, and a large quantity of cloth. "The Negroes went out and begged for the cloth," wrote Mrs. Canning, "saying that it was to make their winter clothes. The cruel destroyers refused to let the Negroes have a single piece." "Well, madam," sneered one of the soldiers, "how do you like the looks of our little fire. We have seen a great many such, within the last few weeks."

Meanwhile, Mr. Canning's interrogators got down to business in the swamp, two miles from the house. "Now, old man, you have to tell us where your gold is hidden." When he replied that his money was in the bank, they cursed and led him to a tree over the path, tied a rope around his neck, threw it over a branch, and lifted him up until his feet were off the ground. Just before he lost consciousness, he was asked again, "now where is your gold?" Another denial led to another jerking off the ground until he nearly suffocated. Lowering him again, they shouted, "now tell us where that gold is or we will kill you, and your wife will never know what has become of you."

"I have told you the truth—I have no gold," he insisted. "I am an old man and at your mercy. If you want to kill me you have the power to do it, but I cannot die with a lie on my lips. I have no gold. I have a gold watch at the house, but nothing else."

"Swing the old Rebel up again!" shouted the leader. This time Mr. Canning heard a sound like rushing water, followed by blindness, before losing consciousness. Finally convinced that he must be telling the truth, the blue-clad gang poured water on his face and brought him back to the house, where they stole his gold watch.

"Oh! the horrors of that night!" wrote Nora Canning. "There my husband lay with scorching fever, his tongue parched and swollen and his throat dry and sore. He begged for water and there was not a drop to be had. The Yankees had cut all the well ropes and stolen the buckets." Mr. Canning continued to suffer for days. "His nose would bleed, and bloody water would ooze from his ears. His eyes were bloodshot and pained him greatly. His tongue was swollen."[21]

At the farm of Sam Hart and his wife, Yankees burned every building except the detached kitchen. The elderly Mrs. Hart was forced to cook for them, after which the soldiers knocked over the table, smashed everything in sight, stole the silver, burned their carriage, and took their horse.[22]

"Missus, for God's sake come out here, and see what you can do about these here devils," said Cornelia Screven's cook, Nancy. Yankee troops had arrived at their Liberty County home and were forcing Nancy to prepare food for them, devouring all she had, and demanding ground cornmeal for their horses.

"Please don't take that meal," said Mrs. Screven, "my children are very hungry, and we have nothing else to eat."

"Damn you," one shouted, "I don't care if you all starve; get out of my way or I'll push you out the door."[23]

James Morgan, a little boy in the village of Sunbury, was ordered by a Federal trooper to bring a burning coal from his

Forager from Sherman's army

fireplace. He watched as they rode to the local church. "I wondered where they were going to build the fire. I knew the church had no chimney. I followed them to the church. They took rails from a fence nearby and built the fire under the stair steps. Soon the church was blazing."[24]

Refugee Eliza Andrews and her party passed through territory only recently visited by Sherman's army. She recounted,

> About three miles from Sparta we struck the "Burnt Country." There was hardly a fence left standing all the way from Sparta to Gordon. The fields were trampled down and the road was lined with carcasses of horses, hogs, and cattle that the invaders, unable either to consume or to carry away with them, had wantonly shot down to starve out the people and prevent them from making their crops. The stench in some places was unbearable. . . . The dwellings that were standing all showed signs of pillage, and on every plantation we saw the charred remains of the gin-house and packing screw, while here and there, lone chimney-stacks, "Sherman's Sentinels," told of homes laid in ashes. The infamous wretches!

Eliza Andrews found a field where the Yankee army had camped weeks earlier. Now "poor people of the neighborhood were wandering over it, seeking for anything they could find to eat, even picking up grains of corn that were scattered around where the Yankees had fed their horses."[25]

A Northern reporter described how Union soldiers would first ransack a house,

> If the spoil were ample, the depredators were satisfied, and went off in peace; if not, everything was torn and destroyed, and most likely the owner was tickled by sharp bayonets into a confession where he had his treasure hid. If he escaped, and was hiding in a thicket, this was prima facie evidence that he was a sulking rebel; and most likely some ruffian, in his zeal to get rid of such vipers, gave him a dose of lead, which cured him of his Secesh tendencies. Sorghum barrels were knocked opened, bee-hives rifled, while their angry swarms rushed frantically about. Indeed, I have seen a soldier knock a planter down because a bee stung him.

> Hogs were bayoneted to bleed; chickens, geese, and turkeys
> knocked over and hung in garlands . . . cows and calves, so
> wretchedly thin that they drop or perish on the first day's
> march, are driven along, or, if too weak to travel, are shot,
> lest they should give aid to the enemy.
>   Should the house be deserted, the furniture is smashed to
> pieces, music is pounded out of four hundred dollar pianos
> with the ends of muskets. Mirrors were wonderfully multi-
> plied and rich cushions and carpets carried off to adorn
> teams and war-steeds. After all was cleared out, most likely
> some set of stragglers wanted to enjoy a good fire, and set
> the house, debris of furniture, and all the surroundings in a
> blaze. This is the way Sherman's army lived on the country.
> They were not ordered to do so, but I am afraid they were
> not brought to task for it much either.[26]

One Illinois soldier in a letter home told of troops being repeatedly warned against pillaging, without it affecting their conduct in the slightest. Almost never enforced, the rule was winked at by nearly all in authority. That same soldier told how his comrades "had a great time last night in Irwinton," for "the citizens had buried a great many things to keep them from the 'vandals' and the boys soon found it out. Hundreds of them were armed with sharpened sticks probing the earth, 'prospecting.' They found a little of everything, and I guess they took it all to the owners."[27] Another Federal, a major, admitted that nothing was done "to prevent these outrages," that prohibitions "are not enforced."[28]

At one home Federal cavalry commander Brig. Gen. Judson Kilpatrick himself ordered troops to vandalize the place and burn surrounding buildings. One slave who tried to put out the flames was threatened with death.[29]

"It was universally understood that men were to help themselves to any thing eatable," one Federal wrote home, adding we "wasted & destroyed all the eatables we couldnt [*sic*] carry off."

> I rather felt sorry for some women who cried & begged so
> piteously for the soldiers to leave them a little and [not to
> take] from such poor places, yet after all I dont [*sic*] know

but extermination is our only means now. They feel now the effect of this wickedness [secession] & who can sympathize very much with them.[30]

The *Macon Telegraph* described the situation in nearby Clinton, where

hundreds of our people are without anything to eat—their stock of cattle and hogs are killed; horses and mules with wagons are all taken off—all through our streets and commons are to be seen dead horses and mules—entrails of hogs and cattle killed, and in many instances, the hams only taken—oxen and carts taken away, so that we are not able to remove the offensive matter—our school houses and most of the churches burned.

Other crimes were far worse. "Atrocities most heinous were committed," the same correspondent wrote, confiding that "female servants [were] taken and violated without mercy."[31]

"Many Negroes were enticed away from homes of comfort to share the uncertain fortunes of a Winter march to the coast," wrote an Augusta journalist, "and then—freedom to starve."[32] Freed blacks following the Federal army were stopped at Ebenezer Creek when troops were ordered to remove a pontoon bridge and leave thousands of these unwanted civilians on the other bank. Attempting to ford the creek, many panicked and subsequently drowned.[33] Sherman defended his corps commander's actions, claiming he merely did not want to lose the pontoon bridge. In a letter to Washington on the matter, Sherman tried to dispel similar rumors "that I burned 500 niggers at one pop in Atlanta, or any such nonsense. I profess to be the best kind of a friend to Sambo."[34] Sherman's anti-black bias was by now becoming notorious. To a friend, the general privately confided that "I like niggers *well enough* as niggers," but only "fools & idiots" promoted their advancement.[35]

A Union officer estimated that his army in marching through Georgia "cleaned up the country generally of almost every thing upon which the people could live." The path of destruction he estimated at being forty miles wide, and "as we have left the country I do not see how the people can live for the next two years."[36] Sherman himself calculated the damage done at one hundred million dollars, 80 percent of which was "simple waste and destruction."[37] But he was sure that any theft from individuals that might have been committed by his troops was "exceptional and incidental."[38]

Chapter 21

"Sometimes the World Seemed on Fire"

Sherman in South Carolina

"I do sincerely believe that the whole United States, North and South, would rejoice to have this army turned loose on South Carolina to devastate that State, in the manner we have done in Georgia," wrote Sherman to Ulysses S. Grant, just prior to his invasion of the Palmetto State.[1] He continued this theme in a letter to Chief of Staff Henry W. Halleck on Christmas Eve 1864.

> We are not only fighting hostile armies, but a hostile people, and must make old and young, rich and poor, feel the hard hand of war. . . . The truth is the whole army is burning with an insatiable desire to wreak vengeance upon South Carolina. I almost tremble at her fate, but feel that she deserves all that seems in store for her.[2]

The men in the ranks shared their commander's hatred for the first Southern state to declare independence. An Ohio private looked forward to destroying "every thing" and predicted to his sister that "ere long you will heare of Shermans army sweeping through S.C. like [a] hericane."[3] South Carolina "will soon reap the whirlwind," wrote one Iowan. "Shermans army are with him to a man and his reputation is their reputation."[4] Another soldier prophesied to a Georgia woman about the punishment that lay in store.

You think the people of Georgia are faring badly, and they are, but God pity the people of South Carolina when this army gets there, for we have orders to lay everything in ashes—not to leave a green thing in the State for man or beast. That State will be made to feel the fearful sin of Secession before our army gets through with it. Here our soldiers were held in check . . . and when they get to South Carolina they will be turned loose to follow their own inclinations.[5]

South Carolinians were not only disturbers of the union, but in the eyes of many Northerners were thought of as inferior human beings. One Federal officer expressed his contempt for those he encountered, referring to them as "white trash" and "not fit to be kept in the same sty with a well to do farmer's hogs in New England."[6] Not surprisingly, an enemy dehumanized would be treated inhumanely.

By February 1, 1865, Sherman had his entire army on the soil of hated South Carolina. Hardeeville first felt their vengeance. A Yankee enlisted man described how the troops disassembled the town in order to use the lumber in building shelters for themselves. "In a few hours a town of half century's growth is thus leveled to the ground."[7] Nor was the local church spared. "First the pulpit and seats were torn out," wrote a sergeant, "then the siding and the blinds were ripped off. Many axes were at work." Soon the spire then the entire building came crashing down. "There goes your damned old gospel shop," shouted one of the vandals.[8]

Searching for valuables, the soldiers repeated many of the tactics they had perfected in Georgia. Nancy DeSaussure of Robertsville told how her elderly uncle was brutalized. Having been suspected of hiding gold, "twice was he hung by them and cut down when unconscious."

After plundering came wholesale destruction. "There was but one fence paling to indicate the site of our little village (Robertville). The church, too, was burned," said Mrs. DeSaussure.[9] The towns of Purysburg, Lawtonville, and McPhersonville also disappeared. "Houses were burned as they were found," reported the correspondent of the *New York*

Herald. "Whenever a view could be had from high ground, black columns of smoke were seen rising here and there within a circuit of twenty or thirty miles."[10]

One bizarre undercurrent of Sherman's devastation came to be known as the "war on dogs." Convincing themselves that Southerners used bloodhounds to track escaped Union prisoners of war, the invaders became obsessed with the notion that all dogs be destroyed. A Federal colonel said that "we were determined that no dogs should escape, be it cur, rat dog or blood hound; we exterminate all." And he saw no need to waste ammunition on the creatures. "The dogs were easily killed. All we had to do was to bayonet them."[11] Some animals, such as cats, "seemed to feel it in the air that something was approaching," observed one woman in the path of Sherman's army. "The watchdog had, in fear, crouched under the dining table," she said, "when a soldier, spying him there, shot him."[12] Another lady living in Barnwell wrote that the first act of the invaders upon breaking into her home was to kill her pet dogs. They barked and growled at the intruders, "but in an instant both were hushed, two sharp pistol reports followed the last growl as the faithful dogs bounded forward only to fall in their tracks, dead." Her terrified children stood by, "shedding silent tears."[13] Sometimes soldiers used the butts of their rifles to kill beloved pets in the presence of children.[14]

Near Barnwell, Mrs. Alfred Aldrich watched helplessly as Yankees made a shambles of her home. When she begged their commander for protection, he claimed to have little control over his troops. "You must remember we are in South Carolina now," he said, "we entered this State with 'gloves off!'"[15] A lady refugee staying in Barnwell remembered how Yankees stole "provisions, clothing, books and an endless variety of things" that they had no use for, leaving these goods in piles around their campgrounds.[16] "They behaved more like enraged tigers, than human beings," said another, "running all over the town, kicking down fences, breaking in doors and smashing glasses." They left Barnwell in flames.[17] Cavalry chief Brig. Gen. Judson Kilpatrick sent a message to Sherman that reportedly amused the general. "We have changed the name of Barnwell to

Burnwell." Kilpatrick's troopers three times set fire to the home of James Courtney, near Montmorenci, and each time the homeowner extinguished the flames. Angered, they shot the fifty-four year old in the leg, leaving him to bleed to death.[18]

Others had good luck in their plundering. One soldier said that a cache of seven thousand dollars in gold was found in the woods by a small party of soldiers. "No notice will be taken of it by any officer."[19] Another recorded that foragers "often found confederate money jewelry & women's dresses." And of course food was always taken from the people. "They cleaned out the country no doubt & probably committed much depredation," he concluded, adding that "we took that even if it left poor women & children to starve as I fear it did in some cases."[20]

An Illinois soldier recorded in his diary that foragers found "plenty of everything we wanted." At one house they loaded wagons with salted meat, meal, flour, sugar, and molasses. Upon leaving, they set fire to a barn filled with cotton and a cotton gin. Hearing the roar of the flames, an old lady came out to see what had been done, fell to her knees, raised her hands, and began fervently to pray. "I did not hear the words she uttered," reported the soldier, "but I do not think she prayed for the Yankees without it was for their ruen. Some of the boys told hir not to take it hard," misspelled the diarist. "That was nothing to what we dun some places."

The same soldier told how they tricked victims into revealing where food was hidden. They would ride to a house and tell the owner that his supply of meat and other food had been found, and they were about to burn it; that if he wanted to save any for his family he must hurry. The thieves would follow the deluded victim, appropriate the provisions for themselves, then offer their thanks "for showing them where it was."[21]

Only occasionally were Northern soldiers forced to stop their outrages—and then only by Confederate forces. Near Aiken, Confederate cavalry met an old man, a Baptist pastor, standing in front of his home, leaning against a fence post for support. "My daughter," he sobbed. "A bunch of Yankees raped her—they just left here." The troopers charged down the road and quickly overtook the party of foragers. "Boys, I know why you do this, but I had nothing to do with it," said one wounded Federal as he begged for his life. The Confederates spared him but executed the others.[22]

There were so many gold watches, rings, chains, silver cups, canes, and similar treasures in the Federal camps that soldiers jested about the plunder. When asked where he got such a valuable item, the soldier's standard reply was that it was presented by a lady "for saving her household goods from destruction." As one expressed it, "a soldier must have his joke."[23]

The cruel jokes extended beyond the borders of the military camps. "One Yankee asked my mother to mend his coat," remembered Mary McMichael of Orangeburg. After she did the work, "He pretended to be very thankful and told her that if she would give him the names of some of her friends in town, he would do all he could to help them. She gave him their names, and he told them that Mrs. McMichael had told him to do them all the harm he could."[24]

Mary Bellinger Fishburne, a young refugee staying in St. Matthews, recounted that one Yankee asked her aunt where her husband was. "He is dead," she replied sadly. "Dead, and in Hell, where you ought to be," replied the Federal.

"The marauders destroyed everything in the way of supplies," continued Mary, "and what they didn't want for themselves they fixed so we couldn't use it. They mixed salt with barrels of syrup and emptied sacks of rice on the floor of the smoke house, flour being served the same fate."[25]

At one home a soldier took a jar of sorghum and filled his canteen. He then spit a wad of tobacco into the jar. The woman complained about his spoiling precious food. "Oh," he said without emotion, "some feller'll come along and taste that sorghum, and think you've poisoned him. Then he'll burn your damned old house."[26]

"Well, it does seem a shame to take every single one," said a soldier, referring to the chickens his comrades had just stolen from a family, "you have this one for dinner." She thanked him for his mercy, with tears streaming from her eyes, as he found some lard for her to fry it in.

"Did you cook the chicken?" he asked, returning later.

"Yes," she replied, "and I gratefully thank you for it. My poor grandchildren are so hungry."

"And I gratefully thank you for it," replied the soldier, grabbing the pan as he left. "I sure got my dinner cooked in a sly way."[27]

At the home of Joe Beard all knew that the invaders were coming. Former slave Fannie Griffin remembered that "the missus told us to put . . . some white peas in a big pot and put a whole ham in it, so that we'd have plenty for the Yankees to eat." Her peace offering was ready. "Then when they came," said Fannie, "they kicked the pot over and the peas went one way and the ham another." When it was discovered that no valuables were to be had, "They got awfully mad and started destroying everything."[28]

"By instinct," insisted former bondsman Andy Brice, a person of his race

> can make up his mind pretty quick 'bout the creed of white folks. . . . Every Yankee I see had the stamp of poor white trash on them. They strutted 'round, big Ike fashion, a bustin' in rooms without knockin', talkin' free to the white ladies, and familiar with the slave gals, ransackin' drawers, and runnin' their bayonets into feather beds, and into the flower beds in the yards.[29]

An Illinois soldier found Orangeburg crowded with women, many of them refugees. Expecting the invaders to burn the town, the women had piled their clothing and bedding out-of-doors. There they stood, some "crying bitterly. Others seemed sullen and independent."[30] The conflagration was not long in coming. Sherman spread the tale that "a Jew merchant" started a fire, but that it "was soon put out."[31] Despite his denial of responsibility, few buildings in Orangeburg survived the brief Federal occupation.

Sherman also seemed unable to explain convincingly what caused Columbia's destruction, except to conclude privately that "it was all right." He probably never read what Henry Halleck had to say in his *Elements of International Law and Laws of War* on the subject of soldiers committing atrocities because they "could not be controlled." This is "no valid excuse," wrote Halleck. "An officer is generally responsible for the acts of those under his orders. Unless he can control his soldiers, he is unfit to command them."[32]

Sherman's out-of-control forces continued their outrages in Winnsboro. Federals camped in and around the Baptist church and staged cockfights inside that house of worship. The Episcopal church was burned. "They stole much that was useless to them," remembered one, "for even Bibles were taken, one, I remember belonging to a little girl." Famed Mount Zion Institute had been converted into a hospital, and there a Confederate soldier named Manigault died just before the invaders arrived and was buried in the Episcopal church-yard. "His new-made grave was dug open," said a witness, "his coffin placed across the grave and split open with an axe, and left so. This was done by those who termed themselves soldiers. 'Hunting for buried treasures' was the reason for such desecration."[33]

Troops "played snowball" in the streets with flour, burned hams and sides of bacon, poured gallons of molasses on the streets, and "fed horses from hats full of sugar," remembered another Winnsboro resident.[34] For days after the army left, hungry women and children scoured the deserted camps for grains of corn uneaten by the horses.[35]

Anne Bell was a slave on a Fairfield District plantation when the Yankees came. "They was full to the brim with mis-chief," she remembered. "Before they left they took every-thing."[36] On the plantation of John Mobley, at nearby Woodward Station, Adeline Jackson was another slave who never forgot the day the invaders arrived. "The Yankees that I remember were not gentlefolks. They stole everything they could take, and the meanest thing I ever see was shoats they half killed, cut off the hams, and left the other parts quiverin' on the ground."[37]

Plantation owner Thomas Lyles at seventy-eight years of

age was far too old to serve in the Confederate army. When enemy troops arrived they found him in bed and unable to walk. "They thought he was shamin', playin' 'possum, so to speak," remembered bondsman Abe Harris. "One of the raiders, a Yankee, came with a lighted torch and said, 'Unless you give me the silver, the gold, and the money, I'll burn you alive.'" The flaming torch was then thrust under the bed. "He replied, 'I haven't many more years to live. Burn and be damned!'" Stunned by the man's bravery—and convinced he concealed no valuables—they spared his life.[38]

At the Durham plantation in Fairfield District there was an old map of the United States displayed on a plaster wall. "One of the soldiers took his bayonet and cut South Carolina out of the map, using such force that he also cut the outline in the wall," recounted owner Margaret Durham. "He said to me, 'Old Woman, that is the way we intend to wipe South Carolina off the map.'" Though it was plundered and all the outbuildings were destroyed, hers was one home in Sherman's path to escape burning. The outline of the state, cut into the wall, remained for generations.[39]

The village of Liberty Hill was filled with refugees when the enemy arrived. "Thousands of Yankees coming in," wrote one lady in her journal, "all robbing and plundering . . . they go down in the cellar and pour kerosene oil, molasses and feathers all together, then stir them up with their bayonets."[40]

At a home in Lancaster an elderly lady was having her morning devotions when the Federals burst in. "Get up old woman, praying will do you no good now, for Sherman's bummers are upon you!" Seeing that she wore gold-rimmed spectacles, one soldier ripped them from her face as his comrades plundered the house. A six-year-old girl hid under a bed, clutching her doll in one hand and a bar of sweet soap in the other. A Yankee dragged her out. "The child was too terror-stricken to cry," said a witness, "but clasped her little doll and her soap fast to the throbbing little heart. The man wrenched both from her and thrust the little one away with such violence that she fell against the bed."[41]

Elizabeth Allston, no more than a schoolgirl, recorded in

her diary the conversation she had with one of the invaders.

"Do you know what you are fighting for?" sneered the Yankee captain.

"Existence," Elizabeth replied.

"We won't let you have it" he grinned. "In four months we'll have the Confederacy on its knees."

Elizabeth fired back. "You must kill every man, woman and child first."

"We'll do it too," said the captain. "At the beginning of this war I didn't care a cent about a nigger, but I'd rather enlist for ten years longer than let the South have her independence. We'll starve you out! Not in one place that we have visited have we left three meals." When it was implied that God still had something to do with events, he replied that "the Almighty has nothing to do with this war!"[42]

A similar sentiment was revealed to the Reverend Dr. John Bachman, a Lutheran minister, who was present when Yankee soldiers forced a female friend to publicly undress, claiming she was hiding jewels under her clothing. They then turned their attention to him, demanding to know where he kept his valuables, though he had none. They cocked pistols and held them to his head, promising to send him "to hell in five minutes" if he did not talk. He told them to go ahead and shoot. A lieutenant with "the face of a demon" kicked the pastor in the stomach and then in the back. Bachman was knocked down as many as eight times during the course of his torture.

"How would you like to have both your arms cut off?" asked the Federal lieutenant, a man who seemed unable to speak a single sentence without swearing. That officer hit the clergyman in the left arm with his sheathed sword, breaking the bone. He then did the same to the right arm. The pain, said Bachman, was "most excruciating."

Bachman's daughter begged for her father's life, pleading that they have mercy on a man who had served his church for decades. "I don't believe in a God, a heaven or a hell," replied the lieutenant. Finally the torturer gave up, allowing the old man to seek medical care.[43]

RAPE

"When the people began to mingle together again," said Margaret Adams after the Yankees moved on,

> each had a thrilling tale to tell, some indeed shocking—of old men who were hung up, time and again, by the neck, to force them to disclose the hiding place of their treasure; of women who had spoken sharply to some of the soldiers, who, for so doing, were tied in chairs in their yards and made to witness the burning of their own houses.[44]

Julia Frances Gott wrote to her sister, telling about "some of the outrages the Yankees have committed." A man named Brice was hung when he refused to tell where valuables were hidden. "They stripped old Mrs. R, Kate's mother, and whipped her," confided Julia. "Wheeler's men [cavalry under the command of Confederate major general Joseph Wheeler] killed sixteen Yanks I hear in retaliation for whipping Mrs. R. Oh Ann, I do think the idea of a Lady's being stripped and whipped by those villains is outrageous, the most awful thing I have heard of."[45]

Confederate brigadier general James Chesnut was informed by Wheeler's cavalrymen of a crime they discovered that was far worse. The home of a family identified as the "M.'s" was found plundered. A party of seven Federals had come upon only Mrs. M and her teenaged daughter at home. They tied up the mother and each then proceeded to rape the daughter. By the time Confederates arrived, the girl was dead and the mother was out of her mind. The Yankees were overtaken on the road by the Southern troopers, who shot them down, cut their throats, and left the bodies with a sign that read, "THESE ARE THE SEVEN."

Ohio sergeant Arthur McCarty had the distinction of being the only Federal soldier to be tried for rape by his own army during the invasion of South Carolina. Three eyewitnesses of the Tenth Illinois testified that a girl in her teens living near Bennettsville was raped by McCarty in the presence of her crying and terrified parents. The sergeant was found guilty and sentenced to two years in prison. Later, petitions from his regiment touting his "soldierly qualities" and letters contradicting the evidence led to a dismissal of his sentence by Pres. Andrew Johnson.[46]

The Confederates also sought some measure of justice for the pillaging. At least two parties of Federal foragers were found dead near the towns of Chester and Feasterville. "Death to all foragers" was the sign posted on the bodies. Sherman assumed they had been killed after capture and sent a letter to Lt. Gen. Wade Hampton, Confederate cavalry commander, threatening to kill Southern prisoners in retaliation. Hampton promised to execute two Federals for every Confederate if Sherman carried out his threat. The South Carolinian—who had lost his own home and those of his family to Federal arsonists—had something to say to the man who was destroying his state and despoiling its people.

> I do not believe my men killed any of yours, except under circumstances in which it was perfectly legitimate and proper that they should kill them. It is a part of the system of the thieves whom you designate as your foragers to fire the dwellings of those citizens whom they have robbed. To check this inhuman system, which is justly execrated by every civilized nation, I have directed my men to shoot down all of your men who are caught burning houses. This order shall remain in force so long as you disgrace the profession of arms by allowing your men to destroy private dwellings. . . .
>
> I do not, sir, question this right [to forage on the country]. But there is a right older, even, than this, and one more inalienable—the right that every man has to defend his home and to protect those who are dependent on him; and from my heart I wish that every old man and boy in my country who can fire a gun would shoot down, as he would a wild beast, the men who are desolating their land, burning their homes, and insulting their women. . . .
>
> You have permitted, if you have not ordered, the commission of these offenses against humanity and the rules of war; you fired into the city of Columbia without a word of warning; after its surrender by the mayor, who demanded protection to private property, you laid the whole city in ashes, leaving amidst its ruins thousands of old men and helpless women and children, who are likely to perish of starvation

and exposure. Your line of march can be traced by the lurid light of burning houses.[47]

Sherman's men had indeed carried out their general's wishes to lay waste to South Carolina. "Even before we came into the State the privations were vastly greater than we had ever supposed," wrote a Federal officer. Now he predicted that the devastated territory "will be abandoned by the inhabitants who will never return."[48] Indeed, some towns disappeared from the map.

"I never saw so much destruction of property before," recorded a Union company commander in South Carolina. "Very few houses escape burning, as almost everybody has run away from before us, you may imagine there is not much left in our track."[49] A Union colonel agreed with that assessment:

We have given South Carolina a terrible scourging. . . . Our army has occupied in moving a belt of from thirty to seventy miles. We have destroyed all factories, cotton mills, gins, presses and cotton; burnt one city, the capital, and most of the villages on our route as well as most of the barns, outbuildings and dwelling houses, and every house that escaped fire has been pillaged.[50]

Plundering in South Carolina

Another soldier concurred that there was "no restraint whatever in pillaging and foraging" while in South Carolina. "Men were allowed to do as they liked, *burn* and *destroy*." But the state "was deserving of it certainly," he was quick to add, as her people were "Enemies of Liberty and free government."[51] An Indiana chaplain agreed that the people of that state were responsible for the atrocities visited upon them. He recounted that the suffering of the people was the "full reward of their folly and crimes," observing that "sometimes the world seemed on fire" as a result of the Union's version of justice.

A Yankee newsman who had seen the March to the Sea summarized Sherman's campaign in South Carolina: "As for wholesale burnings, pillage, devastation, committed in South Carolina, magnify all I have said of Georgia some fifty fold, and then throw in an occasional murder, 'just to make an old, hardfisted cuss come to his senses,' and you have a pretty good idea of the whole thing."[52]

Chapter 22

"And What Do You Think of the Yankees Now?"

The Burning of Columbia

A refugee fleeing Savannah was advised by one Federal officer to avoid the cities and towns of South Carolina—particularly Columbia—since "it was the cradle of secession and must be punished." Another soldier of Sherman's command relished the prospect that "fire & sword" were about to descend, "and there is not one in all the length & breadth of the land to stop our hands."[1] By mid-February 1865 that army arrived on the outskirts of the capital, a city by then made up almost entirely of women, children, old men, and slaves.[2]

To slow the enemy's advance, bridges over the Congaree, Broad, and Saluda Rivers had been burned by retreating Confederates. Early on February 16, Union artillery unlimbered on the bank of the Congaree and began firing on downtown. Sherman seemed unconcerned about any Southern soldiers who might still be in the city but noted "quite a number of Negroes . . . near the burned depot." The general ordered his battery commander to aim at these civilians, as they "were appropriating the bags of corn and meal which we wanted."[3] In all, Federal artillery threw 325 rounds of shot and shell into the city that morning. "You could see the cannons every time they would fire," remembered a youthful observer, "and hear the shells whistle through the air. Some of them would explode in the air and others would not."[4] Miraculously, only two civilians were killed by the bombardment.[5]

So much for Sherman's denial

Just before leaving the city, Confederate major general Wade Hampton was asked if bales of cotton piled in the streets should be destroyed by fire to avoid confiscation by the enemy. "No," he replied, "the wind is high; it might catch something and give Sherman an excuse to burn this town."[6]

After Confederate forces evacuated, about 9 A.M., Mayor Thomas Jefferson Goodwyn met the advancing Federals and surrendered his city, asking for—and receiving—promise of protection for persons and property.[7] Upon entering Columbia some Union officers permitted their men to be given liquor, and soldiers started looting stores and igniting the cotton. Flames were soon extinguished by municipal firefighters. One Iowa soldier said that when he arrived, "The cotton had been drenched and the street flooded with water and, to all appearances, the fire entirely subdued." That was fortunate, for about 2 P.M. troops began to pass the time by slashing and bayoneting hoses.[8]

Throughout the day, reported a witness, "robbery was going on at every corner—in nearly every house." Purses, watches, hats, boots, overcoats—any item of value—were taken from victims, white or black. "Nor were these acts [entirely] those of common soldiers," he noted. "Commissioned officers, of a rank so high as that of a colonel, were frequently among the most active."[9] At one home soldiers in their search for hidden valuables stabbed knives into a mattress between terrified children, "thinking that the children were put there as a blind."[10] Countless women had earrings ripped from bleeding ears. "I have myself seen a lady with the lobes of both ears torn asunder," wrote a foreign diplomat.[11] A bedridden, dying woman had rings removed from her fingers. "In several cases, newly made graves were opened," remembered a witness, "the coffins taken out, broken open, in search of buried treasure, and the corpses left exposed."

Yankee troops relieved themselves in the rooms of Columbia homes, defiling crockery, even urinating on beds.[12] On one street a Union soldier, "seeing some children playing with a beautiful little greyhound, amused himself by beating its brains out."[13] Churches were pillaged. At the Catholic convent "soldiers drank the sacramental wine and profaned with fiery draughts of vulgar whiskey the goblets of the communion service. Some went off reeling under the weight of priestly robes, holy vessels and candlesticks."[14]

"Columbia is a doomed city!" hissed one.[15] "And what do you think of the Yankees now?" taunted another. "We mean to wipe you out! We'll burn the very stones of South Carolina." One victim observed, "To inspire terror in the weak . . . seemed to these creatures a sort of heroism."[16]

That afternoon smoke was seen rising from suburban residences belonging to prominent "rebels," properties specifically targeted by Federals. "It was surprising to see the readiness with which these incendiaries succeeded in their work of destruction," wrote local educator Sophie Sosnowski. "They had hardly passed out of sight when columns of smoke and flames rose to bring the sad news that another home had been sacrificed to the demon of malice and arrogance."[17]

Then came sundown. "Four rockets have gone up," a lady told her family, "one at each corner of the town, all at the same moment." These rockets were recognized as a signal for general destruction.[18] One observer said that at the signal "troops from the various camps began to pour into the city like locusts."[19] Another remembered "the hitherto deserted street filled with a throng of men, drunken, dancing, shouting, cursing wretches, every one bearing a tin torch or a blazing lightwood knot."[20] One saw soldiers as they "went about with matches, turpentine and cotton, with which they fired the houses."[21] Sixteen-year-old Emma LeConte described how "Sumter Street was brightly lighted by a burning house so near our piazza that we could feel the heat. By the red glare we could watch the wretches walking—generally staggering—back and forth from the camp to the town—shouting—hurrahing—cursing South Carolina—swearing—blaspheming—singing ribald songs."[22] According to a refugee from Charleston, "demons in human shape were leaping fences with torches and steeped cotton. . . . They danced with fearful shrieks and curses, and their forms shone out hideously in numbers on all sides in the light of our flaming homes."[23] As victims reached the streets, wrote a woman in her diary, "we were greeted by, 'How do you like secesh now,' 'Columbia is skedaddling,' 'Columbia is on a picnic,' and curses too fearful to be entered in my book."[24]

"What we experienced that night is indescribable," said another. "At one time the air was so hot I felt I would suffocate. We walked under an arch of fire, meeting terrified children and distracted mothers."

"I trust I shall never witness such a scene again—drunken soldiers, rushing from house to house, emptying them of their valuables, and then firing them," wrote Northern reporter David Conyngham. Of those troops ostensibly assigned to keep order, "I did not once see them interfering." "The frequent shots on every side told that some victim had fallen," he continued, recounting that he had himself been fired at for attempting to save a man from murder.[25]

"On came the flames," wrote a witness,

> driven by a fierce wind and augmented by the cruel torches of the fiends, who unrelentingly applied them to building after building, as they rushed from block to block. The

Columbia on fire

streets were as bright as day, and the air was rent with the screams and cries of distress, mingled with infant wails, and the demon yells of the tormenters. Who can picture that scene, except to compare it with the lower regions?[26]

Seventy-two-year-old Agnes Law placed her trust in four "well-behaved and sober" soldiers standing guard over her home.

When the city began to burn I wished to remove my furniture [she said], they objected and said my house was in no danger. Not long afterward these guards themselves took lighted candles from the mantelpiece and went up stairs. . . . My sister followed them up-stairs, but came down very soon to say, "They are setting the curtains on fire." Soon the whole house was in a blaze. When those who set fire up-stairs came down they said to me, "Old woman, if you do not mean to burn up with your house you had better get out of it."

"I have been for over fifty years a member of the Presbyterian church," concluded Mrs. Law. "I cannot long live. I shall meet General Sherman and his soldiers at the bar of God, and I give this testimony against them in the full view of that dread tribunal."[27]

Rev. Peter J. Shand, assisted by a servant, tried to save the silver communion service of Trinity Episcopal Church. They were stopped by soldiers who stole it along with that clergyman's watch.

On Washington Street, the Methodist pastor twice smothered fires set at his church. Soon he saw that the parsonage was burning. Quickly he wrapped his child in a blanket and they escaped to the street only to witness flames breaking out anew at the church. Angered that he had tried to frustrate their arson, one Federal ripped the blanket away and threw it into the conflagration. "Damn you!" he snapped, "if you say a word, I'll throw the child after it."[28]

Witnesses saw soldiers torching the Catholic convent. "What do you think of God now?" they shouted to the nuns. "Is not Sherman greater? Do you think now you are sanctified? We are as sanctified as you."[29]

Sunrise revealed a landscape of smoldering ruins. Much of the city, including the main business district, was gone. Thousands of homeless civilians huddled against the cold in gardens, parks, and cemeteries.[30] "Oh, it was a pitiable sight," wrote a Federal private, "to see the mothers with helpless children, out of doors, their houses burnt to the ground." But he was not surprised at the fate of "secessionist" Columbia. "Our soldiers always said if they entered the place, they would burn it and they did."[31]

"It is true our men have burnt Columbia," Sherman told Mayor Goodwyn the morning after, "but it was your fault." Columbia's civilian population, he insisted, had made his men drunk.[32] "I know that the general judgment of the country is that no matter how it began," Sherman privately confided to his brother, "it was all right."[33] In his official report he pointed the finger at Wade Hampton, claiming the Confederate general left burning cotton in the streets. Later Sherman confessed that he charged Hampton only "to shake the faith of his people in him," inadvertently admitting at the same time that it was indeed his own troops who "utterly ruined Columbia."[34]

"Sherman may have issued no order," concluded one historian of the city's destruction, "but his failure to control his men constituted probable tacit consent."[35] "*There is no doubt whatsoever,*" wrote another, "*that Union soldiers were to blame for what happened, some with intent, others by default in their drunken stupor.*"[36] Incredibly, there are still those who downplay Federal responsibility.[37] "If a transaction that occurred in the presence of forty or fifty thousand people can be successfully falsified," concluded witness Edwin J. Scott, "then all human testimony is worthless."[38]

Chapter 23

"We Must Make the Thing Pay Somehow"

Sherman in North Carolina

Like most Northerners, William T. Sherman profoundly misunderstood Southern "Unionism." Upon entering North Carolina he issued an order to Brig. Gen. Judson Kilpatrick that the cavalry chief "deal as moderately, and fairly by North Carolinians as possible, and fan the flame of discord already subsisting between them and their proud cousins of South Carolina. There never was much love between them."[1] Indeed, for decades North Carolinians had distrusted Palmetto State disunionism and initially viewed secession as unnecessary and unwise. But everything changed on April 15, 1861, when Lincoln called for troops to invade the new Confederacy. Unionism in North Carolina was not unconditional; her people would not countenance coercion. "I can be no party to this wicked violation of the laws of the country and to this war upon the liberties of a free people," replied North Carolina's governor, John Ellis. "You can get no troops from North Carolina." Delegates, most former Unionists, met in convention and voted unanimously for secession.[2] During the course of the war at least 120,000 North Carolinians donned the Confederate uniform to fight for independence, and a third gave their lives in that cause.[3]

Sherman's admonition to deal "moderately" was generally ignored, and he must have quickly realized that these people were not about to embrace his Union. "Poor North Carolina will have a hard time," the general wrote privately after a month in that state, "for we sweep the country like a swarm of locusts. Thousands of people may perish, but they now realise that war means something else than vain glory and boasting."[4]

Monroe and Wadesboro were among the first to "have a hard time" at the hands of Kilpatrick's troopers. Episcopal bishop of North Carolina, Thomas Atkinson, was threatened with death if he did not give up his watch, horse, and possessions. Another Anson County man was robbed of his watch and money, and the next band of Federals to arrive at his home demanded the very same items. They killed him when he could not produce them.[5] At a nearby home Yankees chopped furniture to pieces with an axe and scattered feathers from pillows on a bedroom floor then poured on buckets of molasses and stirred thoroughly. Ten wagons filled with unlucky refugees were overtaken and their possessions captured.[6]

Anson County resident Esther Alden grieved about the suffering of her neighbors as well as over what the Yankees did to the animals.

> It is like some horrid nightmare. When I shut my eyes I see nothing but creatures and human beings in agony. The poor suffering horses! Some fortunately dead and out of their misery, others groaning in death pains, some with disabled limbs freely hobbling about to glean a blade of grass; the cows and oxen slaughtered and left to rot! I counted eight beautiful calves lying dead in one pen; many times we saw two or three lying dead side by side![7]

Teenager Janie Smith was appalled by the Federals' obsession with sparing no living thing, however insignificant. She called them "fiends incarnate." At her home an old hen "played sick and thus saved her neck, but lost all her children," said Janie. Chicks were chased by the soldiers, who "would run all over the yard to catch the little things to squeeze to death."[8]

In Fayetteville the Yankees destroyed one thousand horses and mules they had no use for. There were two killing grounds:

one a field on the bank of the Cape Fear River, the other a corral in town. It took hours to shoot them all. Trying to run, some of the terrified animals plunged into the river. Most were left where they fell, with no effort made by Federals to dispose of the carcasses as the troops abandoned the town. "They were burned," wrote a witness, "and you may try to imagine the odor, if you can."[9]

A dozen miles outside Fayetteville, at the home of Duncan Murchinson, Kilpatrick's cavalrymen charged into the bedroom of a small girl desperately sick with typhoid. They were looking for items to steal but found nothing and were asked to leave. "Go ahead boys," growled an officer. "Do all the mischief you can." Seventy-year-old Mr. Murchinson was dragged to the swamp and assaulted while vandals destroyed furniture, slashed family portraits, and poured molasses into the piano. The little girl died while the troopers were still in her home. Fortunately, Federal horses left a little uneaten corn on the ground, for that was all the family had to live on after the invaders moved on.[10]

A woman who lived near Fayetteville told of Yankees murdering two citizens. "They hung up three others and one lady, merely letting them down just in time to save life, in order to make them tell where their valuables were concealed; and they whipped—stripped and cowhided—several good and well known citizens for the same purpose." She went on to recount that soldiers killed "every living thing, even to our pet dog," before breaking tools and burning the fences. After stealing or destroying all the food they could find, one Federal asked her sarcastically what she would live on. "Upon patriotism," she replied. "I will exist upon the love of my country as long as life will last, and then I will die as firm in that love as the everlasting hills." The interview concluded when he departed with "a fiendish chuckle."[11]

Josephine Worth, a young girl at the time, remembered that "the sky was lurid with the flames from the burning homesteads, but it has passed into a proverb that Sherman's route could be traced by solitary chimneys where happy homes once stood." At her uncle's place, four miles from Fayetteville, they vandalized everything. "Even the family Bible was not sacred," wrote Josephine. "One of them opened it and spread it over a mule's back and rode off on it for a saddle." At least a servant was able to find a small quantity of precious cornmeal at a friend's home. "My aunt made some bread from the meal and as she was cooking it before the fire, a scamp sitting by kept spitting over and around it. 'Please don't spit on my bread,' said my aunt. With that, he spat directly into it—the bread intended to feed our hungry little children."[12]

One Yankee told of torching turpentine mills in the Fayetteville vicinity, something "which certainly made the handsomest fires I ever saw, especially the smoke as it rolled up in great black volumes was splendid. We blazed our way well through here."[13] Homes went up in flames too.[14] Churches were used as barracks, vandalized, and desecrated.[15] In all cases, factories were slated for destruction.

In Fayetteville, city fathers gathered with the mayor and town board to ask an audience, begging that the conqueror spare the cotton mills. They pled their case, meeting with Sherman in the home he occupied as headquarters, and argued that the people needed the employment those mills provided. It probably went unsaid—but understood by all—that the war was nearly over in any case. Sherman let them finish before dismissing them with three sentences: "Gentlemen, Niggers and cotton caused this war, and I wish they were both in Hell. On Thursday those mills will be blown up. Good morning."[16]

One witness described what happened in a single neighborhood. "J.P. McLean was hung up by the neck three times and shot at once, to make him disclose hidden valuables. W.T. Horne, Jesse Hawley, and Alexander McAuthor, were all hung up until nearly dead. John Waddill was shot down and killed in his own house."[17]

The home of Georgia Hicks was on the Goldsboro and Wilmington Road, near the village of Faison, from where she was able to learn much of the behavior of Union troops as they passed through. A relative, Rachel Pearsal, "aged and ill, was thrown from her bed to the floor, so that they could look for valuables they thought hidden there." Georgia's father, Dr.

James H. Hicks, was asked by Federal soldiers to come and treat one who was sick.

> He was carried far away and when he was brought back later, he had the appearance of a man that had almost seen death. These ruffians hung him by the neck twice, in their endeavor to secure information as to hidden valuables. They finally released their victim who refused to divulge his secrets. He never recovered from this terrible shock.[18]

"They haven't recognized their deliverers yet," observed Clara Maclean, referring to terrified black children cowering in silence as Yankee soldiers plundered the home. An elderly lady there had the front of her dress ripped open in their search for hidden coins. A watch and other items were grabbed from the pocket of another. One of the troopers claimed that they had come after hidden "rebels." "And after watches," shot back Clara. "Oh, well!" he smiled. "We must make the thing pay somehow."[19]

Cornelia Spencer of Goldsboro recognized the approach of Sherman's army, "heralded by columns of smoke which rose from burning farm-houses on the south side of the Neuse [River]."

> One of the first of General Sherman's own acts, after his arrival, was of peculiar hardship. One of the oldest and most venerable citizens of the place [Richard Washington], with a family of sixteen or eighteen children and grandchildren, most of them females, was ordered on a notice of a few hours, to vacate his house, for the convenience of the General himself, which of course was done. The gentleman was nearly eighty years of age, and in very feeble health.[20]

The devastation the Union army had wreaked upon North Carolina did not go unrecognized by the Federals who had overseen the destruction. "I never before had an idea of how desolate our army leaves a country," remarked a Federal colonel, "and we thought we were letting North Carolina off easy. It is terrible the wretched, suffering condition the people are in."[21]

Gen. Robert E. Lee surrendered his army on April 9. The Confederate capital of Richmond had been abandoned six days earlier. Gen. Joseph E. Johnston ordered his men to lay down their arms on April 26. It was not until three days later that Sherman's troops in North Carolina were required to cease their "pillaging and marauding" of civilians.[22]

Chapter 24

"Marse General Sherman Said War Was Hell"

Abuse of African-Americans

"They asked me who my master was," recounted Fanny Carr on her confrontation with the Yankee soldiers. "I said I had no master, that I was a free colored woman." Fanny Carr, a resident of Alexandria, Louisiana, though born a slave had been free for more than twenty years. The widow stayed in her own home on the outskirts of town with a grown daughter, Catherine. Catherine, also free, worked as a domestic for a neighbor, Mrs. Thomas C. Manning. The Carrs kept farm animals for their own use. Their frame dwelling was proudly maintained and filled with prized household possessions. Fanny cherished the watch left by her husband, and young Catherine took special pride in her bonnets and jewelry. Mother and daughter were respected members of the community. Thomas Manning, associate justice of the state supreme court, characterized them as "truthful and industrious people."

The blue-clad invaders arrived in Alexandria in mid-March 1864 and immediately began plundering the town. "On seeing me they asked who I was," said Fanny. When she tried to make them understand that she was free, they called her a liar. When she said that the house belonged to her and to no one else, "they cursed me and called me a liar again, and said niggers could not own property in this State."

"They commenced pillaging the house," said Fanny. "I begged them to stop." It was no use. Taken from the home were her silverware, plates, tablecloths, sheets, and mirrors, along with her and Catherine's clothes. Expensive woolens and linens were stolen, "and my husband's gold watch," said Fanny, "which I minded more than the clothes." All their food supply disappeared, along with the poultry and a hog. A store of lumber she had accumulated was chopped to pieces. The vandals then proceeded to pull down the house itself, even taking bricks from the chimney.

Fanny was literally left with nothing but the clothes on her back. She later saw her stolen garments being given by the troops "to one of their colored women and a white woman who came off one of the gunboats in the river just in front of the town."

Catherine had been at work when the invaders came and did not get home until the next day. Furious over the theft and destruction, she stormed to the headquarters of Brig. Gen. Joseph Mower. "The Yankees said we should not have our things back; that they knew they were not ours, for colored people were not allowed to own so much property down here. I told them they *did* belong to us," insisted Catherine. She then asked Col. William T. Shaw for provisions since his soldiers had taken all that she and her mother had to live on. "They wanted me to go away with them." When she refused, Shaw sarcastically replied "that if I wanted to stay down here I could get the Rebels to feed me." She told him the rebels *would* feed her, and she would *not* go off with Yankees.[1]

In the spring of 1863 Federals marching up Bayou Teche stopped to plunder the mansion of the late Dubriel Olivier. Olivier, a wealthy planter and slave owner, was reported to have raised and equipped at his own expense a Confederate company two years earlier. Now his widow, Aimee, defiantly met the invading Yankees and ordered them away. "Where is your master?" laughed a soldier. Assuming she was the maid, they insisted she have more respect for white people. It finally dawned on the intruders that she was indeed mistress of the plantation, that Dubriel and Aimee Olivier were *gens de couleur libre*—"free people of color."

One Connecticut officer expressed shock at seeing so many

French-speaking, light-skinned blacks, individuals with the audacity to "call themselves Americans." "These are not the former slaves," he pointed out in a letter home, "but the former masters." St. Landry Parish's free African-American population totaled 1,596 in 1858, and some of those individuals prospered as the owners of sugar plantations and the masters of slaves. "Neither the color of their skin nor their special status mattered to the Yankees," wrote an historian. "The cattle, horses and sugar of Alphonse and A.D. Meuillon, Alexandre Lemelle, Jules Frilot, Sosthene Auzenne and Zenon Rideau, all free men of color, were taken and consumed just as readily as the goods seized from [white neighbors]."[2]

It was not uncommon for even slaves to accumulate some savings in gold or silver coin, and these little hoards were targeted by invading Yankees. A favorite trick in Louisiana was for a soldier to claim that "Old Abe" or their commanding general had personally made him responsible for collecting valuables, that the owner would receive the money back once it and the liberated slave were transported beyond reach of the "rebels." One Louisiana slave named Jerry "deposited" his five hundred dollars' worth of savings into a safe aboard a Union ship. "He was referred by the officer to some other officer who he said had the key," it was reported later, "and by him to some other officer who was the one that received it, and by him to some other, and so on in endless continuity." When the Federal army and supporting riverboats withdrew, Jerry went along in a futile hope of somehow reclaiming his savings.[3]

During the Federal invasions of western Louisiana in 1863 and 1864, thousands of slaves were encouraged to leave their homes and follow the troops. "We use uneducated horses and mules taken from the enemy," Union commander Maj. Gen. Nathaniel Banks was overheard to say. "Why not negroes?" Former slaves might end up in the ranks of his army, laboring on confiscated plantations for wages, or employed as prostitutes. All too often, women, children, and those too old or sick to work were simply abandoned by their liberators. "They were afraid to return to their former masters," wrote one historian, "because many of them had participated in the destruction and plunder before leaving, and because of the wildly exaggerated stories circulated by Union soldiers that Confederate pickets were shooting down runaways on sight."

In late June 1863, after the Union army left Berwick's Bay, a horrendous discovery was made. On the banks of Bayou Ramos, some seven miles from Brashear, scores of dead and dying runaway slaves were found huddled in a thicket. Decomposing bodies were all around, while survivors "were crouched to the earth with their heads sunk between their knees, or lying with upturned faces and gazing vacantly at the air," according to a witness. Nearby was a building, part of a local sugar plantation belonging to a man named Sanders, that housed hundreds more. Dr. George Hill, for forty years an Opelousas physician, described what he saw there:

> The scene which then and there presented itself can never be effaced from my memory. On the right hand female corpses in a state of nudity, and also in a far advanced decomposition. Many others were lying all over the floor, many speechless and in a dying condition.
>
> All appeared to have died of the same disease: bloody

Refugee train

flux. The floor was slippery with blood, mucus and feces. The dying, and all those unable to help themselves, were lying with their scanty garments rolled around their heads and breasts. . . . clouds of flies, such as I never saw before, would immediately rise and settle down again on all parts of the dying. In passing through the house a cold chill shook my frame. . . .

As I passed from the house I met with a Negro man of my own, who informed me that he had lost his wife and two children. I asked him if his friends—the Yankees—had not furnished him with medicine. He said, "No, and if they had, I would not have given it to my family as all who took their medicine died in twelve hours from the time of its being given."

Commissioners for the state of Louisiana took testimony and issued a report on the conduct of the invading troops. Though black survivors were almost unanimous in their belief that Federals tried deliberately to poison them, the report concluded this not to be true. Still, "we know the Negroes religiously *believe* what they state." A careful examination of the facts concluded that between May 21 and June 29, 1863, two thousand of those who ran away with the army had perished.

The Federal Red River Campaign the following year made matters even worse. Often crowded into "contraband camps," it was inevitable that disease and starvation would take a terrible toll. Children were separated from parents. Those who eventually returned "all concur in representing their misery and destitution as deplorable, and the mortality as frightful." In Rapides Parish alone it was estimated that between May 1863 and March 1864, eight thousand slaves left their homes to follow the Union army and that one-half died.[4]

In Mississippi, the conduct of the Federals toward the slaves was much the same as evidenced in Louisiana. "They had taken all the money from every Negro on the plantation," wrote Susan Dabney Smedes of Hinds County, Mississippi, recounting a raid on her home by United States troops. One crippled sixty-three-year-old slave was a preacher named Isaac. "Uncle Isaac had buried eighty dollars in gold,—the savings of years," continued Mrs. Smedes. "This he was made to unearth. He had lately bought a new silver watch, for which he had paid forty dollars. This was taken from him."

When Federals came through the neighborhoods of Guntown and Saltillo, Mississippi, they committed the usual theft and destruction of property. But they were particularly zealous to take all the slaves they could, presumably needing their labor. Rev. James Agnew wrote in his journal that "the Yankees shot two of [Thomas] Burris's Negroes down in the yard because they would not go with him."[5]

"I won't trust niggers to fight yet," wrote William T. Sherman in the spring of 1863, "but don't object to the Government taking them from the enemy, & making such use of them as experience may suggest." In Union-occupied Tennessee the army impressed blacks and put them to work at hard labor or hired them out to private contractors who often literally starved them. When the Federal army decided to build fortifications around Nashville, they made a surprise raid on blacks living there and "gathered them in from barber-shops, kitchens, and even churches," wrote one of their kidnappers. "Many who traded Southern owners and overseers for Yankee bosses," observed an historian, "very quickly discarded any lingering notions about Northern benevolence." Those put to work for the army were poorly fed, not properly sheltered, and paid little or nothing. Death was common. One Union army officer in Nashville admitted that "colored men here are treated like brutes." A Davidson County civilian saw blacks working in an army camp and thought them "the most miserable wretched looking creatures I ever saw"; those who became sick were treated as if "they were so many dogs."

Nashville's blue-clad conquerors were feared by black civilians. When Ohio soldiers were unable to find seats in a crowded theater one evening in September 1862, they invaded the "Negro gallery" and began shoving patrons out of their way. "In ten minutes," read a report, "every Negro had been badly beaten and ejected, some of them being thrown entirely down the stairs, from the top to the bottom." After the performance, troops went about the streets of the city attacking every African-American in sight.

Robbery was common, as was sexual abuse of black women by Yankee soldiers. A U.S. cavalry regiment recruited from among East Tennessee Unionists and described by one girl as "the meanest men I ever saw" rode into Gallatin in May 1864 and began a reign of terror. They torched two newly established schools for black children, murdered one freedman, and swore they would—as soon as they could—kill every black in town.[6]

Liberty County in rural southeast Georgia had in antebellum times an unusually large number of free blacks, and some had gradually and laboriously accumulated substantial property. Many of those still in bondage had also managed to earn money with their skilled labor and purchased stock and grew crops of their own.[7] When Sherman's troops came through in 1864 everything was stolen or destroyed, whether owned by planters or by hardworking slaves. A white diarist recorded that black women were particularly threatened by the invaders. "These men were so outrageous at the Negro houses, that the Negro men were obliged to slap at their horses [causing them to bolt] for the protection of their wives, and in some instances they rescued them from the hands of these infamous creatures." One historian concluded that in Liberty County, "indiscriminate confiscation of black property, and other anti-Negro acts committed by Sherman's army, had a corrosive effect on the enthusiasm with which many had welcomed him."[8]

In May 1864, Sherman began his invasion of northern Georgia. A black nurse living on a plantation near Kingston found herself in the path of that army. "They've took everything I had," she sobbed, telling her young mistress that her animals had been killed and her savings stolen by the soldiers. "Honey, I never knowed a Yankee that wasn't mean as dirt. They would skin a flea for his hide an' tallow. Everybody say the Yankees goin' to free us. Like a fool I believe 'em, an' now this is what they do. I might a-knowed it. What can you spec from a hog but a grunt."[9]

Callie Elder, a young slave girl, told how Union soldiers stole money belonging to her master that had been entrusted to the care of her father. The thieves then victimized the slaves. "Grandma was a churnin' away out on the back porch and she had a ten dollar gold piece what she didn't want them soldiers to steal, so she dropped it in the churn," said Callie. "Them Yankees poured that buttermilk out right there on the porch floor and got grandma's money."[10]

Camilla Jackson's master, physician Peter Hoyle, took his slaves and fled the approach of Sherman's army. They returned to find that all the slave quarters had been leveled, but Dr. Hoyle's home inexplicably was still standing. The slaves stayed in the master's house until their own homes could be rebuilt.[11]

Mrs. Dolly Burge, a native of Maine, was living with her family and their servants on the Madison road, nine miles east of Covington, Georgia, when Sherman's army arrived. A number of young black boys were forced by the soldiers "at the point of the bayonet" to come with them. Mrs. Burge recorded the kidnapping in her journal.

> One (Newton) jumped into the bed in his cabin & declared himself sick, another crawled under the floor, a lame boy he was, but they pulled him out & placed him on a horse & drove him off. Mid, poor Mid, the last I saw of him, a man had him going round the garden looking as I thought for my sheep as he was my shepherd. Jack came crying to me, the big tears coursing down his cheeks saying they were making him go. I said: "Stay in my room," but a man followed in, cursing him & threatening to shoot him if he did not go. Poor Jack had to yield. James Arnold, in trying to escape from a back window, was captured & marched off. Henry, too, was taken, I know not how or when, but probably when he & Bob went after the mules. . . .
>
> My poor boys, my poor boys, what unknown trials are before you. . . . Their parents are with me now & how sadly they lament the loss of their boys. Their cabins are rifled of every valuable, the soldiers swearing that their Sunday clothes were the white people's. . . . Poor Frank's chest was broken open, his money & tobacco taken. He has always been a money-making & saving boy. Not infrequently his crop brought him five hundred dollars & more.[12]

Yankee soldiers robbed the home of Allie Travis in Covington. She and a female servant were standing in the yard, watching as the blue-clad troops marched by. Suddenly the slave girl "recognized some of her clothing in the hands of a soldier returning to the street. She immediately investigated the matter, and found that they had broken open her house and were appropriating all that she prized. She soon filled the yard with her shrieks and lamentations."

"What's the matter with that nigger?" growled one of the Union troops.

"Your soldiers," replied Allie, "are carrying off everything she owns, and yet you pretend to be fighting for the Negro."[13]

Nora M. Canning and her husband, Judge Canning, returned to their plantation home in Jefferson County, Georgia, only to find that Federal cavalry had burned everything, even destroying their crops. "The poor Negroes had fared no better than we had," wrote Mrs. Canning. "Their *friends* had stolen everything from them as well as from us . . . even their shoes were taken from their feet. Their chickens had all been killed and their bed and bedding all carried off."

Mrs. Canning and her husband noticed one of their slaves "sitting on her door steps swaying her body back and forth, and making a mournful noise, a kind of moaning, a low sorrowful sound, occasionally wringing her hands and crying out."

"Master," she said, raising her head, "What kind of folks these here Yankees? They won't even let the dead rest in the grave."

"What do you mean?" asked Judge Canning.

"You know my child what I bury last week? They take him up and left him on top of the ground for the hog to root. What you think of that, sir?"

"Her story was true," wrote Mrs. Canning.

> We found that the Vandals had gone to the graveyard and, seeing a new made grave, had dug down into it and taken up the little coffin containing a dead baby, no doubt supposing treasure had been buried there. When they discovered their mistake, they left it above ground, as the poor mother expressed it, "for the hog to root."[14]

Mrs. Alfred Proctor Aldrich of The Oaks plantation near Barnwell, South Carolina, hid her valuables herself. Assuming that the servants knew the whereabouts of the silver, one Union soldier put a rope around the neck of a black man named Frank and threatened him with death if he did not reveal the hiding place. Mrs. Aldrich only learned of his ordeal later. "Each of the three times that this man suspended poor Frank in the air he would let him down and try to make him confess," she said. "Not knowing anything, of course he could not give the coveted information. Frank's neck remains twisted to this day."[15]

"Daddy" John Gardener, in Orangeburg, South Carolina, was similarly threatened by soldiers searching for loot. "The Yankees put a pistol to his head," remembered a witness, "telling him he knew where his master had buried certain things they wished to get hold of." Though he was standing over the place where the hidden treasures were stashed, he told them, "Please *God,* boss, you'll have to shoot. I can't tell you anything about my master's affairs."[16]

"Where is all the white people's gold and silver?" soldiers demanded of slaves at another South Carolina home. "My Ma said she didn't know," remembered Adeline Grey, a young girl at the time. "'You do know!' they said, and choked her till she couldn't talk." When the soldiers left, they made Adeline's mother come with them, forced to carry a sack of stolen meat. Her children rejoiced to see her return later that night. "She said she slipped behind, and slipped behind," said Adeline, "and when she came to a little pine thicket by the side of the road, she darted into it, dropped the sack of meat they had her carryin', and started out for home."[17]

Soldiers also kidnapped twelve-year-old slave Sam Rawls of Lexington County, South Carolina.

> I was in marse's [John Hiller's] yard. They come up where the boss was standing . . . grabbed him and hit him. They burned his house, stole his stock, and one Yankee stuck his sword to my breast and said for me to come with him or he would kill me. O' course I went long. They took me as far as Broad River, on t'other side of Chapin; then turned me loose

and told me to run fast or they would shoot me. I went fast and found my way back home by watching the sun.[18]

"What did the Yankees do when they come?" asked former slave Andy Marion.

They tied me up by my two thumbs and try to make me tell where I hid the money and gold watch and silver, but I swore I didn't know. Did I hide it? Yes, so good it was two years befo' I could find it again. I put everything in a keg, went into the woods, spaded the dirt by a pine stump, put the keg in, covered it up with leaves and left it. Sometime after, we looked for it, but couldn't find it. Two years later, I had a mule and cart in the woods. The mule's foot sunk down into the old stump hole and there was the keg, the money, the silver and the watch. Master was mighty glad that I was a faithful servant, and not a liar and a thief like he thought I was.[19]

All too often, threatened slaves had to comply with the demands of the robbers. Cureton Milling remembered that two Yankees rode up to the plantation kitchen, demanding that servants disclose where valuables were hidden. "Tell us or we'll beat you worse than you ever got from the lash of the patrollers," he quoted one soldier as saying. "They was as good as their words," he continued, "they got down and grabbed us and made us tell all we knew."[20]

"They'd go through the house an' take everything," said Daphney Wright, a young slave woman of Hardeeville, South Carolina. "Take from the white, an' take from the colored, too. Take everything out the house! They take from my house . . . But I didn't have anythin' much . . . Had a little pork an' a week's supply of rations."[21]

"Mom" Hester Hunter's family was threatened and terribly frightened by the invaders. "Oh, my God, them Yankees never bring nothin' but trouble and destructiveness when they come here," she said.[22]

Penny Alsbrook may have felt fear, but certainly did not show it. When Yankee soldiers demanded something to eat for themselves and water for their horses, "She coolly informed them," said a witness, that if they wanted anything, "they could get down and get it, she never had waited on no poor white trash and never intended to." She stood by in silence as soldiers invaded her kitchen, "got the bread tray for the horses to eat out of, broke up the dishes, knocked down the stove, broke out the window panes and did, as she expressed it, 'everything devilish they could.'" The vandalism continued, but Penny "stood by and watched them without a word, until one of them started to pick the baby of the household up in his arms. She tore at him like a tiger and clawed his face and hands and grabbed the baby and ran."[23]

"First thing they look for was money," remembered bondsman Lewis Evans. "They put a pistol right in my forehead and say, 'I got to have your money, where is it?'"

> There was a gal, Caroline, who had some money; they took it away from her. They took the geese, the chickens and all that was worth takin' off the place, stripped. Took all the meat out of the smoke-house, corn out the crib, cattle out the pasture, burnt the gin-house and cotton. When they left, they shot some cows and hogs and left them lyin' right there. There was a awful smell 'round there for weeks after.[24]

Anna Hasell Thomas of Mount Hope plantation near Ridgeway, South Carolina, remembered of the blue-clad invaders:

> [They] had treated the Negroes shamefully; stolen the little silver some had, killed, eaten or stolen their fowls, and they had some heads to prove how many had been killed. One of the slave girls, they had dressed in their own regimentals and carried her off. They had left the slaves nothing eatable except cow peas, which they had probably never seen before, and did not know that they were eatable.[25]

A Federal officer confessed that soldiers would "plunder the houses of the blacks of the last mouthful of food and every valuable and take pleasure in insulting and molesting them when they meet them."[26] That was the experience of slave girl Violet Guntharpe. "The Yankees sho' threwed us in the briar batch, but we weren't bred and born there like the rabbit."

Violet went on to describe her home built of logs. Slaves had cows to give them milk, horses and mules to help them work the crops. They had hogs "fattenin' on hickory nuts, acorns, and shucked corn to give us meat and grease; the sheep with their wool, and the cotton in the gin house was there to give us clothes . . . but when them Yankees come and take all that away, all we had to thank them for was a hungry belly, and freedom." She remembered black babies "suckin' their thumbs for want of sumpin' to eat; mind you 'twas winter time too. Lots of children died, as did old folks, while the rest of us scour the woods for hickory nuts, acorns, cane roots, and artichokes, and seine the river for fish." Violet could not help but note that "the worst" of the liberated slaves left to follow the invading army[27]—a decision most of them would soon come to regret.

Sophie Sosnowski, headmistress of a school for girls near South Carolina's capital city, was shocked when one party of Yankee soldiers decided to harangue them. "One among them, made a regular stump speech, in which he endeavored to demonstrate that this country was destined only for the white man, and that the Indian, as well as the Negro had to be, or in the course of events would be, exterminated."[28]

Madame Sosnowski was appalled, too, by the treatment black women received from the invading troops at the home she had taken refuge in during the Federal occupation of Columbia. "The scenes enacted at that dwelling in connection with the Negro servants are not fit for female pen to dwell upon. . . . At last the [black men] themselves became thoroughly disgusted, and . . . vowed vengeance for the base treatment their women had been subjected to."[29]

One black woman, a servant of Columbia minister Peter Shand, was raped by seven soldiers of the United States Army. She then had her face forced down into a shallow ditch and was held there until she drowned. William Gilmore Simms reported how "regiments, in successive *relays*," committed gang rape in Columbia on scores of slave women.[30]

"What does this mean, boys?" asked Sherman, coming upon a young African-American man dead on a Columbia street.

Maj. Gen. William T. Sherman

"The damned black rascal gave us his impudence, and we shot him," calmly replied a soldier.

"Well, bury him at once!" ordered Sherman. "Get him out of sight!"

When asked about the matter, Sherman said that "we have no time for courts-martial and things of that sort!"[31]

One Union army officer described the train of black refugees that followed Sherman's army in South Carolina.

> It was a curious sight to see some fifty vehicles of every description from the fancy carriage . . . to the heavy farm cart loaded with Negroes of every description, sex, age and hue, carrying with them household fixtures, etc., living by foraging as our army does, and having to take what is left after the army is served and of course suffering the most painful privation. I have seen them dying on the road in wagons, carts, etc. . . . I am grieved to see many of our soldiery treat them with the greatest unkindness.[32]

Mary Chesnut recorded in her diary the horrific news that the bodies of eighteen black women had been discovered on the Sumter District plantation of her niece Minnie Frierson and husband, James. Each had been stabbed in the chest with a bayonet. "The Yankees were done with them!" wrote Mrs. Chesnut. "These are not rumours but tales told me by the people who *see* it all."[33]

North Carolina slaves suffered at the hands of the invaders as well. "They came from ever'where but outen the ground and down outen the sky," remembered Martha Graham. "They took all the corn outen the crib and the things we'd stored. When they left, we didn't have nothin'." Her mother was in the house straining milk when a Yankee barged in, helped himself to it, and just as quickly left. Seconds later a shot rang out. "They was killing our turkey," said Martha. "Darn your black skin," a soldier shouted at another North Carolina home, "give me the watch in your pocket!" A blind slave woman had her new dress stolen.[34]

"Them Yankees done a lot of mischief," said former slave and North Carolinian Tiney Shaw. "I know because I was there." Besides their "robbin', plunderin', and burnin' up everything," Tiney remembered that "a whole lot of darkies what ain't never been whipped by the master got a whuppin' from the Yankee soldiers."[35]

North Carolina plantation mistress Cornelia Phillips Spencer remarked how "unfortunate Negroes were the severest sufferers, they being stripped of their all, and beginning a new life of freedom, began it without even the little savings and personal property accumulated in slavery."[36]

Four-year-old Charles Dickens remembered that his mother had a shoulder of meat that she hid under a mattress in their slave cabin. "When the Yankees left, she looked for it; they had stole the meat and gone."[37]

Another small slave boy, Blount Baker, recounted that the Yankees "talked mean to us an' one of them said that we niggers were the cause of the war. 'Sir,' I said, 'folks that are wanting a war can always find a cause.' He kicked me in the seat of the pants for that, so I hushed."[38]

The Yankees would regret their run-in with eight-year-old Ida Lee Adkins. Ida lived on the plantation of her master, Frank Jeffries, and his wife, Mary Jane, near Louisburg, North Carolina. Mr. Jeffries was too old to serve in the Confederate army but met the invading Yankees with characteristic defiance and as a result was tied up on his porch.

"I was scared near 'bout to death," said Ida, "but I ran to the kitchen an' got a butcher knife, an' when the Yankees wasn't lookin', I tried to cut the rope an' set Marse Frank free. But one of them blue devils seed me an' come running."

"What are you doin', you black brat!" shouted the Federal. "You stinkin' little alligator bait!"

"He snatched the knife from my hand," continued Ida, "an' told me to stick out my tongue, that he was going to cut it off. I let out a yell an' run behind the house."

As the Yankees continued to pillage her master's home, Ida had an idea.

'Bout that time I seed the bee gums [hives] in the side yard. . . . I run an' got me a long stick an' turned over every one of them gums. Then I stirred them bees up with that stick till they was so mad I could smell the poison. An' bees! You ain't never seed the like of bees. They was swarmin' all over the place. They sailed into them Yankees like bullets, each one madder than the other. They lit on them horses till they looked like they was alive with varmints. The horses broke their bridles an' tore down the palings an' lit out down the road. But that running was nothin' to what them Yankees done. They bust out cussin', but what did a bee care about cuss words! . . . The Yankees forgot all about the meat an' things they done stole; they took off down the road on a run, passin' the horses. The bees was right after them in a long line.

With the invaders gone, Master Jeffries was quickly freed and most of the plunder recovered. "Ida Lee," said Mrs. Jeffries, "We want to give you something you can keep so you'll always remember this day, and how you run the Yankees away."

"Then Miss Mary Jane took a plain gold ring off her finger an' put it on mine," a seventy-eight-year-old Ida Lee Adkins told a newspaper reporter in 1936. "An' I been wearin' it ever since."[39]

By 1936, eighty-seven-year-old Henry D. Jenkins of Fairfield County, South Carolina, had become a substantial landowner and a respected citizen. He grew up a slave on the Sumter District plantation of Joseph Howell. He told an interviewer what he remembered of the Federal invasion.

When the Yankees come, what they do? They did things they ought not to have done and left undone the things they ought to have done. Yes, that 'bout tells it. One thing you might like to hear. Mistress [Sara Howell, wife of plantation owner Joseph Howell] got all the money, the silver, the gold and the jewels, and got the well digger to hide them in the bottom of the well. Them Yankees smart. When they got there, they asked for the very things at the bottom of the well. Mistress wouldn't tell. They held a "court of enquiry" in the yard; called slaves up, one by one, good many. Must have been a Judas 'mongst us. Soon a Yankee was let down in the well, and all that money, silver, gold, jewelry, watches, rings, brooches, knives and forks, butter-dishes, waiters, goblets, and cups was took and carried 'way by an army that seemed more concerned 'bout stealin', than they was 'bout the Holy War for the liberation of the poor African slave people. They took off all the horses, sheep, cows, chickens, and geese; took the seine and the fishes they caught, corn in crib, meat in smoke-house, and everything. Marse General Sherman said war was hell. It sho' was. Maybe it was hell for some of them Yankees when they come to die and give account of the deeds they done in Sumter and Richland Counties.[40]

Notes

Chapter 1

1. U.S. War Department, comp., *War of the Rebellion: A Compilation of the Official Records of the Union and Confederate Armies,* ser. 1, vol. 24, pt. 3 (Washington, D.C.: Government Printing Office, 1880-1901), 943 (hereafter cited as *O.R.*).

2. F. J. P. Veale, *Advance to Barbarism* (Appleton, Wis.: C. C. Nelson Publishing Co., 1953), 66.

3. Ibid., 62, 76.

4. Richard Shelly Hartigan, *Lieber's Code and the Law of War* (Chicago: Precedent Publishing, 1982), 4.

5. Richard M. Weaver, "Southern Chivalry and Total War," in *The Southern Essays of Richard M. Weaver,* ed. George M. Curtis III and James J. Thompson (Indianapolis: Liberty Press, 1987), 168-69.

6. Richard M. Weaver, *The Southern Tradition at Bay: A History of Postbellum Thought,* ed. George Core and M. E. Bradford (New Rochelle, N.Y.: Arlington House, 1968), 215.

7. Telford Taylor, *Nuremberg and Vietnam: an American Tragedy* (Chicago: Quadrangle Books, 1970), 155.

8. James M. McPherson, *Battle Cry of Freedom: The Civil War Era* (New York: Oxford University Press, 1988), 619.

9. *The Lysander Spooner Reader* (San Francisco: Fox & Wilkes, 1992), 49.

10. Thomas J. DiLorenzo, *The Real Lincoln: A New Look at Abraham Lincoln, His Agenda, and an Unnecessary War* (New York: Three Rivers Press, 2003), 258.

11. *O.R.*, ser. 1, vol. 19, pt. 2, 602.

Chapter 2

1. Louis S. Gerteis, *Civil War St. Louis* (Lawrence: University Press of Kansas, 2001), 88; John McElroy, *The Struggle for Missouri* (Washington, D.C.: The National Tribune Co., 1909), 50; Donald L. Gilmore, *Civil War on the Missouri-Kansas Border* (Gretna, La.: Pelican Publishing Co., 2006), 109.

2. *O.R.*, ser. 3, vol. 1, 82-83.

3. Christopher Phillips, *Damned Yankee: The Life of General Nathaniel Lyon* (Columbia: University of Missouri Press, 1990), 131, 136, 153.

4. Ibid., 176-78.

5. *O.R.*, ser. 1, vol. 3, 7-8.

6. Phillips, *Damned Yankee,* 176.

7. Ibid., 181-82; *O.R.*, ser. 1, vol. 3, 4.

8. Phillips, *Damned Yankee,* 164, 185, 187; Gerteis, *St. Louis,* 104.

9. *O.R.*, ser. 1, vol. 3, 4-5, 7.

10. Gerteis, *St. Louis,* 107-9, 350.

11. *O.R.*, ser. 1, vol. 3, 9.

12. Phillips, *Damned Yankee,* 193, 209.

13. Walter Brian Cisco, *Taking a Stand: Portraits from the Southern Secession Movement* (Shippensburg, Pa.: White Mane Books, 1998), 112.

14. *O.R.*, ser. 1, vol. 8, 431-32, 446.

15. Richard S. Brownlee, *Gray Ghosts of the Confederacy: Guerrilla Warfare in the West, 1861-1865* (Baton Rouge: Louisiana State University Press, 1958), 169.

16. *O.R.*, ser. 1, vol. 8, 476-78, 611-12.

17. *Military Laws of the Confederate States* (Richmond: J. W. Randolph, 1863), 65; O.R., ser. 1, vol. 13, 726-28, 835; John Ellis, *A Short History of Guerrilla Warfare* (New York: St. Martin's Press, 1976), 86.

18. *O.R.*, ser. 1, vol. 13, 506, 518; Bruce Nichols, *Guerrilla Warfare in Civil War Missouri, 1862* (Jefferson, N.C.: McFarland & Co., 2004), 104.

19. Brownlee, *Gray Ghosts,* 158-59, 164-65.

20. *O.R.*, ser. 1, vol. 22, pt. 1, 868-69.

21. Nichols, *Guerrilla Warfare,* 189.

22. *O.R.*, ser. 1, vol. 13, 791.

23. *O.R.*, ser. 1, vol. 22, pt. 2, 42-43.

24. Brownlee, *Gray Ghosts,* 161-62.

25. Carolyn M. Bartels, *Bitter Tears: Missouri Women and Civil War, Their Stories* (Independence, Mo.: Two Trails Press, 2002), 45-47.

26. Brownlee, *Gray Ghosts,* 160-61; Nichols, *Guerrilla Warfare,* 157, 173.

27. Brownlee, *Gray Ghosts,* 176-77.

28. Ibid., 174-75; *O.R.*, ser. 1, vol. 22, pt. 1, 319.

29. Brownlee, *Gray Ghosts,* 159; Nichols, *Guerrilla Warfare,* 79.

30. Gilmore, *Civil War,* 134-35, 139-40, 142.

31. Nichols, *Guerrilla Warfare,* 7, 9, 79.

32. Ibid., 90, 120, 125, 148, 151, 154, 156, 173, 184, 192; Preston Filbert, *The Half Not Told: The Civil War in a Frontier Town* (Mechanicsburg, Pa.: Stackpole Books, 2001), 142.

33. Brownlee, *Gray Ghosts,* 170-71; Bartels, *Bitter Tears,* 39; *O.R.*, ser. 1, vol. 48, pt. 1, 644.

34. Bartels, *Bitter Tears,* 67-68.

35. Nichols, *Guerrilla Warfare,* 100-2.

36. Ibid., 109, 125, 151.

37. Brownlee, *Gray Ghosts,* 173.

Chapter 3

1. Brownlee, *Gray Ghosts,* 118-19; Edward E. Leslie, *The Devil Knows How to Ride* (New York: Random House, 1996), 194-97; "Collapse of Union Jail, Kansas City, Missouri," The Missouri Partisan Ranger Web site: http://www.rulen.com/partisan/collapse.htm (accessed 13 August 2005). There are several variant spellings of the girls' names.

2. Brownlee, *Gray Ghosts,* 119-21; *O.R.,* ser. 1, vol. 22, pt. 2, 460-61.

3. Albert Castel, "Order No. 11 and the Civil War on the Border," *Missouri Historical Review* 57 (July 1963). Civil War St. Louis Web site: http://www.civilwarstlouis.com (accessed 13 August 2005).

4. Leslie, *Devil,* 254.

5. Carey S. Bliss, ed., "An Unpublished War Letter of General William T. Sherman," *The Huntington Library Quarterly* 8, no. 1 (November 1944): 108.

6. *O.R.,* ser. 1, vol. 22, pt. 2, 471-72.

7. Ibid., 473.

8. Leslie, *Devil,* 258, 260-61.

9. Castel, "Order No. 11"; Bartels, *Bitter Tears,* 147, 182.

10. Leslie, *Devil,* 262.

11. Castel, "Order No. 11."

12. Leslie, *Devil,* 264; Bartels, *Bitter Tears,* 118.

13. Leslie, *Devil,* 262; Larry Sullivan, "The Lone Jack Massacre" and "The Exile of Nancy Cave," Erazo Family Web site: http://erazo.org (accessed 4 March 2005).

14. Joanne Chiles Eakin, *Tears and Triumph: Order No. 11* (Independence, Mo.: privately published, 1996), 102.

15. Castel, "Order No. 11."

Chapter 4

1. Cisco, *Taking a Stand,* 85, 109, 111.

2. Walter T. Durham, *Nashville, the Occupied City: The First Seventeen Months—February 16, 1862, to June 30, 1863* (Nashville: The Tennessee Historical Society, 1985), 52.

3. Ibid., 143.

4. *O.R.,* ser. 1, vol. 7, 671.

5. Durham, *Nashville,* 57.

6. *O.R.,* ser. 2, vol. 4, 289.

7. Durham, *Nashville,* 48, 75, 152.

8. Ibid., 71, 86, 154-55.

9. Stephen V. Ash, *Middle Tennessee Society Transformed, 1860-1870: War and Peace in the Upper South* (Baton Rouge:

Louisiana State University Press, 1988), 91, 101-2.

10. Alfred Leland Crabb, *Nashville: Personality of a City* (Indianapolis: The Bobbs-Merrill Co., 1960), 62.

11. Durham, *Nashville,* 64, 76-77, 148, 168, 247-49.

12. Ibid., 240, 244-45.

13. Peter Maslowski, *Treason Must Be Made Odious: Military Occupation and Wartime Reconstruction in Nashville, Tennessee, 1862-65* (Millwood, N.Y.: KTO Press, 1978), 64.

14. Durham, *Nashville,* 168-69.

15. Ibid., 27.

16. *O.R.*, ser. 1, vol. 23, pt. 2, 56-57.

17. *O.R.*, ser. 1, vol. 5, 451-52.

18. Durham, *Nashville,* 262-63.

19. Michael R. Bradley, *With Blood and Fire: Life Behind Union Lines in Middle Tennessee, 1863-1865* (Shippensburg, Pa.: Burd Street Press, 2003), 99-100.

20. Durham, *Nashville,* 152, 164-65, 181.

21. *O.R.*, ser. 1, vol. 20, pt. 2, 72.

22. Durham, *Nashville,* 260.

23. Ibid., 233.

24. Ibid., 261-62.

25. Ibid., 172.

26. Henry Steele Commager, ed., *Documents of American History,* vol. 1 (New York: Appleton-Century-Crofts, 1968), 429.

27. Maslowski, *Treason,* 91-92.

28. Bradley, *Blood and Fire,* 59-60.

29. Margaret B. Paulus, comp., *Papers of General Robert Huston Milroy,* vol. 4 (n.p.: privately published, 1965), 91-92.

30. Bradley, *Blood and Fire,* 110.

31. Ash, *Middle Tennessee,* 87, 89, 153-54.

32. Durham, *Nashville,* 180.

33. Ash, *Middle Tennessee,* 89, 159.

34. Maslowski, *Treason,* 133.

35. *O.R.*, ser. 1, vol. 31, pt. 3, 262.

36. Monroe Seals, *History of White County, Tennessee* (Spartanburg, S.C.: The Reprint Co., 1974), 73-74.

37. *O.R.*, ser. 1, vol. 34, pt. 1, 353.

38. *O.R.*, ser. 1, vol. 32, pt. 2, 38; Bradley, *Blood and Fire,* 53.

39. Durham, *Nashville,* 223-24.

40. Bradley, *Blood and Fire,* 76-79.

41. Ibid., 115-17, 120-21, 141.

Chapter 5

1. John T. Goolrick, *Historic Fredericksburg: The Story of an Old Town* (Richmond: Whittet & Shepperson, 1922), 70, 75, 91; George A. Bruce, *The Twentieth Regiment of Massachusetts Volunteer Infantry 1861-1865* (Boston: Houghton, Mifflin and Company, 1906), 206; Francis Augustin O'Reilly, *The Fredericksburg Campaign: Winter War on the Rappahannock* (Baton Rouge: Louisiana State University Press, 2003), 124.

2. Goolrick, *Historic Fredericksburg,* 46-47.

3. O'Reilly, *Fredericksburg Campaign,* 124.

4. Josiah Marshall Favill, *The Diary of a Young Officer: Serving with the Armies of the United States During the War of the Rebellion* (Chicago: R. R. Donnelley & Sons Company, 1909), 210-11.

5. Thomas Francis Galwey, *The Valiant Hours,* ed. W. S. Nye (Harrisburg, Pa.: The Stackpole Company, 1961), 58.

6. Matthew J. Graham, *The Ninth Regiment New York Volunteers (Hawkins' Zouaves): Being a History of the Regiment and Veteran Association from 1860 to 1900* (New York: E.P. Cody & Co., printers, 1900), 386.

7. George C. Rable, *Fredericksburg! Fredericksburg!* (Chapel Hill: University of North Carolina Press, 2002), 177.

8. Graham, *Ninth Regiment,* 385-86.

9. Rable, *Fredericksburg!* 178, 182, 184.

10. Robert Garth Scott, ed., *Fallen Leaves: The Civil War Letters of Major Henry Livermore Abbott* (Kent, Ohio: Kent State University Press, 1991), 155.

11. Charles H. Banes, *History of the Philadelphia Brigade: Sixty-Ninth, Seventy-First, Seventy-Second, and One Hundred and Sixth Pennsylvania Volunteers* (Philadelphia: J. B. Lippincott & Co., 1876), 138.

12. Graham, *Ninth Regiment,* 384.

13. O'Reilly, *Fredericksburg Campaign,* 118-19, 123.

14. John Michael Priest, ed., *From New Bern to Fredericksburg: Captain James Wren's Diary* (Shippensburg, Pa.: White Mane Publishing Company, Inc., 1990), 97.

15. Bruce, *Twentieth,* 210.

16. "Disgrace of Our Army," *The Old Guard* 1, no. 9 (September 1863): 234.

17. Rable, *Fredericksburg!* 181.

18. O'Reilly, *Fredericksburg Campaign,* 126.

19. Goolrick, *Historic Fredericksburg,* 47.

Chapter 6

1. Stephen Chicoine, *John Basil Turchin and the Fight to Free the Slaves* (Westport, Conn.: Praeger, 2003), 59.

2. Faye Acton Axford, ed., *The Journals of Thomas Hubbard Hobbs* (University, Ala.: University of Alabama Press, 1976), 228, 230-31.

3. *O.R.,* ser. 1, vol. 10, pt. 1, 877.

4. S. S. Canfield, *History of the 21st Regiment Ohio Volunteer Infantry, in the War of the Rebellion* (Toledo: Vrooman, Anderson & Bateman, 1893), 46.

5. Chicoine, *Turchin,* 88.

6. *O.R.,* ser. 1, vol. 10, pt. 1, 878.

7. Henry J. Haynie, *The Nineteenth Illinois* (Chicago: M. A. Donohue & Co., 1912), 166.

8. Chicoine, *Turchin,* 65-67.

9. *O.R.,* ser. 1, vol. 10, pt. 1, 878.

10. Chicoine, *Turchin,* 64-65.

11. Ibid., 1-5, 12, 18.

12. Ibid., 67; Roy Morris, Jr., "The Sack of Athens," *Civil War Times Illustrated* 24, no. 10 (February 1986): 28.

13. *O.R.,* ser. 1, vol. 16, pt. 2, 274-75.

14. *O.R.,* ser. 1, vol. 10, pt. 2, 212.

15. Morris, "Athens," 29.

16. *O.R.,* ser. 1, vol. 16, pt. 2, 273-75; Chicoine, *Turchin,* 91-92, 99-100.

17. Morris, "Athens," 30.

18. Frederick D. Williams, ed., *The Wild Life of the Army: Civil War Letters of James A. Garfield* (n.p.: Michigan State University Press, 1964), 121.

19. Chicoine, *Turchin,* 102.

20. Morris, "Athens," 31.

21. *O.R.,* ser. 1, vol. 16, pt. 2, 276-77.

22. Chicoine, *Turchin,* 97-98.

23. Ibid., 99, 115.

24. Morris, "Athens," 32.

Chapter 7

1. Chester G. Hearn, *When the Devil Came Down to Dixie: Ben Butler in New Orleans* (Baton Rouge: Louisiana State University Press, 1997), 69; James Parton, *General Butler in New Orleans* (Boston: Ticknor and Fields, 1866), 346.

2. John D. Winters, *The Civil War in Louisiana* (Baton Rouge: Louisiana State University Press, 1963), 125-26; Dick Nolan, *Benjamin Franklin Butler: The Damnedest Yankee* (Novato, Calif.: Presidio Press, 1991), 2, 11; Hearn, *Devil Came Down,* 2.

3. Hearn, *Devil Came Down,* 180.

4. Ibid., 2-3.

5. W. C. Corsan, *Two Months in the Confederate States: An Englishman's Travels Through the South* (Baton Rouge: Louisiana State University Press, 1996), 17.

6. Parton, *General Butler,* 325-26.

7. Ibid., 327.

8. Winters, *Louisiana,* 132.

9. *O.R.,* ser. 1, vol. 10, pt. 2, 531.

10. *O.R.,* ser. 1, vol. 15, 743.

11. Hearn, *Devil Came Down,* 105.

12. C. Vann Woodward, ed., *Mary Chesnut's Civil War* (New Haven: Yale University Press, 1981), 343.

13. Hearn, *Devil Came Down,* 134, 136-37.

14. Parton, *General Butler,* 352.

15. Hearn, *Devil Came Down,* 86; Winters, *Louisiana,* 131-32, 134-36, 140.

16. *O.R.*, ser. 2, vol. 4, 883-84.

17. Hearn, *Devil Came Down,* 169-70; Corsan, *Two Months,* 24-25; *O.R.*, ser. 2, vol. 4, 881.

18. Hearn, *Devil Came Down,* 173-74.

19. Robert Werlich, *"Beast" Butler* (Washington, D.C.: Quaker Press, 1962), 58-59.

20. Winters, *Louisiana,* 137-38, 140; Hearn, *Devil Came Down,* 181-82, 185-86, 196, 223.

21. Hearn, *Devil Came Down,* 3, 217.

22. Werlich, *"Beast" Butler,* 78-79.

23. Hearn, *Devil Came Down,* 105, 138, 221.

24. *O.R.*, ser. 1, vol. 15, 906.

Chapter 8

1. John W. Gordon, *South Carolina and the American Revolution: A Battlefield History* (Columbia: University of South Carolina Press, 2003), 97.

2. Mark V. Kwasny, *Washington's Partisan War, 1775-1783* (Kent, Ohio: Kent State University Press, 1996), xii, 339.

3. *O.R.*, ser. 1, vol. 17, pt. 1, 144-45.

4. *O.R.*, ser. 1, vol. 13, 742-43.

5. *O.R.*, ser. 1, vol. 17, pt. 2, 288-89.

6. Harry S. Stout, "Discrimination: The Civilians' Civil War," from Beecher Lectures 2005. Yale University Web site: www.yale.edu/divinity (accessed 1 February 2006).

7. *O.R.*, ser. 2, vol. 4, 568, 573.

8. Ibid., 702, 724.

9. Charles W. Wills, *Army Life of an Illinois Soldier,* comp. Mary E. Kellogg (Carbondale: Southern Illinois University Press, 1996), 136, 145.

Chapter 9

1. Cisco, *Taking a Stand,* 111.

2. "Virginia County Vote on the Secession Ordinance, May

23, 1861." New River Notes Web site: http://www.newriver-notes.com/va/vasecesh.htm (accessed 26 December 2005).

3. "West Virginia Statehood." West Virginia Division of Culture and History Web site: http://www.wvculture.org/history/statehoo.html (accessed 26 December 2005).

4. "Virginia County Vote."

5. Ibid.

6. Jonathan A. Noyalas, "My will is absolute law': General Robert H. Milroy and Winchester, Virginia," (master's thesis, Virginia Polytechnic Institute and State University, 2003), 4, 6-7.

7. Margaret B. Paulus, comp., *Papers of General Robert Huston Milroy,* vol 4 (n.p.: privately published, 1965), 83, 85-86, 88.

8. *O.R.,* ser. 3, vol. 2, 944.

9. *O.R.,* ser. 2, vol. 5, 808-10.

10. *O.R.,* ser. 3, vol. 2, 943-44.

11. Ibid., 944.

12. Ibid., 943-44; *O.R.,* ser. 3, vol. 3, 15.

13. *O.R.,* ser. 3, vol. 3, 8.

14. Ibid., 8-10.

15. "Virginia County Vote."

16. *O.R.,* ser. 2, vol. 5, 811.

17. Paulus, *Papers,* 58; *O.R.,* ser. 3, vol. 3, 10-12, 15-16.

18. *O.R.,* ser. 1, vol. 21, 1102.

Chapter 10

1. Noyalas, "Milroy," 1.

2. "Virginia County Vote."

3. Noyalas, "Milroy," 19, 21, 32.

4. Cornelia Peake McDonald, *A Woman's Civil War: A Diary, with Reminiscences of the War, from March 1862,* ed. Minrose C. Gwin (Madison: University of Wisconsin Press, 1992), 153.

5. Ibid., 120, 123, 132, 139; Michael G. Mahon, ed., *Winchester Divided: The Civil War Diaries of Julia Chase and Laura Lee* (Mechanicsburg, Pa.: Stackpole Books, 2002), 79.

6. Noyalas, "Milroy," 39, 42.

7. McDonald, *Diary,* 120, 138.

8. Noyalas, "Milroy," 36, 39.

9. McDonald, *Diary,* 117.

10. Noyalas, "Milroy," 27-28.

11. Ibid., 26, 34-35.

12. Roger U. Delauter, Jr., ed., *Winchester in the Civil War* (Lynchburg, Va.: H. E. Howard, 1992), 50; Mahon, *Winchester Divided,* 89-90.

13. Ezra J. Warner, *Generals in Blue: Lives of the Union Commanders* (Baton Rouge: Louisiana State University Press, 1972), 326.

14. Noyalas, "Milroy," 53-54.

Chapter 11

1. E. Milby Burton, *The Siege of Charleston 1861-1865* (Columbia: The University of South Carolina Press, 1970), 251-59.

2. *Born in Slavery: Slave Narratives from the Federal Writers' Project, 1936-1938,* South Carolina, vol. 14, pt. 3, 216. Library of Congress Web site: http://memory.loc.gov/ammem/snhtml/snhome.html (accessed 9 March 2005).

3. W. Chris Phelps, *The Bombardment of Charleston, 1863-1865* (Gretna, La.: Pelican Publishing Co., 2002), 34, 64-65, 107.

4. Burton, *Siege,* 259.

5. *Columbia Daily South Carolinian,* 20 January 1864.

6. Burton, *Siege,* 258-59.

7. Phelps, *Bombardment,* 151.

8. *O.R.,* ser. 1, vol. 44, 741, 797, 799.

Chapter 12

1. John D. Winters, *The Civil War in Louisiana* (Baton Rouge: Louisiana State University Press, 1963), 235-36.

2. David C. Edmonds, ed., *The Conduct of Federal Troops in Louisiana During the Invasions of 1863 and 1864: Official Report Compiled from Sworn Testimony Under the Direction of*

Governor Henry W. Allen Shreveport, April 1865 (Lafayette, La.: Acadiana Press, 1988), 22-23, 97.

3. David C. Edmonds, *Yankee Autumn in Acadiana* (Lafayette, La.: Acadiana Press, 1979), 181-83.

4. Edmonds, *Conduct,* 58-59.

5. Ibid., 28-33, 36-37, 39.

6. Ibid., 5, 63.

7. *O.R.*, ser. 1, vol. 15, 373.

8. Cecil D. Eby, Jr., ed., *A Virginia Yankee in the Civil War: The Diaries of David Hunter Strother* (Chapel Hill: University of North Carolina Press, 1961), 169; Edmonds, *Conduct,* 40.

9. Edmonds, ed., *Conduct,* 51, 57.

10. Ibid., 86, 90-92.

11. Edmonds, *Yankee Autumn,* 348-49; Edmonds, *Conduct,* 39-40, 42-43.

12. Edmonds, *Conduct,* 48-49, 51, 198; *O.R.*, ser. 2, vol. 6, 710.

13. Winters, *Louisiana,* 236.

14. Edmonds, *Conduct,* 34, 79-81, 89.

15. Ibid., 82-85, 88-89.

16. Ibid., 55-57, 60-61, 63-64, 66.

17. Edmonds, *Yankee Autumn,* 248-50, 317.

18. Winters, *Louisiana,* 335.

19. *O.R.*, ser. 1, vol. 34, pt. 3, 307.

20. *O.R.*, ser. 1, vol. 34, pt. 1, 581.

21. Edmonds, *Conduct,* 174-76.

22. Ibid., 162.

23. Ibid., 151, 159, 178-79, 182-83; Winters, *Louisiana,* 373-74.

24. Winters, *Louisiana,* 387.

Chapter 13

1. *Articles of War, U.S. Statutes at Large,* 2 (1789-1848). Ninety-first Pennsylvania Volunteer Infantry Web site: http://freepages.military.rootsweb.com/~pa91/cfawar.html (accessed 12 May 2005).

2. *Articles of War for the Government of the Armies of the Confederate States* (Charleston: Evans & Cogswell, 1861).

Smithsonian National Museum of American History Web site: http://americanhistory.si.edu/militaryhistory/collection/object.asp?ID=77 (accessed 12 May 2005).

3. Daniel Walker Hollis, *South Carolina College,* vol. 1 of *The University of South Carolina* (Columbia: The University of South Carolina Press, 1951), 180, 192; Richard Shelly Hartigan, *Lieber's Code and the Law of War* (Chicago: Precedent Publishing, 1983), 5-6, 83.

4. Hartigan, *Lieber's Code,* 8, 13; *The Lieber Code of 1863.* The Home of the American Civil War Web site: http://www.civilwarhome.com/liebercode.htm (accessed 17 May 2005).

5. Hartigan, *Lieber's Code,* 109.

6. John F. Marszalek, *Commander of All Lincoln's Armies: A Life of General Henry W. Halleck* (Cambridge: The Belknap Press of Harvard University Press, 2004), 3, 193.

7. *Instructions for the Government of Armies of the United States in the Field (Lieber Code),* 24 April 1863. International Committee of the Red Cross Web site: http://www.icrc.org (accessed 2 March 2005).

8. Hartigan, *Lieber's Code,* 120-21.

9. *Instructions for the Government of Armies.*

Chapter 14

1. *O.R.*, ser. 1, vol. 38, pt. 5, 68; Michael D. Hitt, *Charged with Treason: Ordeal of 400 Mill Workers During Military Operations in Roswell, Georgia, 1864-1865* (Monroe, N.Y.: Library Research Associates, 1996), 120.

2. Hitt, *Charged,* 17, 39.

3. *O.R.*, ser. 1, vol. 38, pt. 5, 76-77.

4. Hitt, *Charged,* 50, 89.

5. Dale L. Walker, *Mary Edwards Walker: Above and Beyond* (New York: Tom Doherty Associates, 2005), 158; Hitt, *Charged,* 114, 123.

6. Hitt, *Charged,* 96, 114, 129.

7. Frances Thomas Howard, *In and Out of the Lines: An Accurate Account of Incidents During the Occupation of Georgia*

by Federal Troops in 1864-65 (Cartersville, Ga.: Etowah Valley Historical Society, 1998), 43-44.

8. Hitt, *Charged,* 121.

9. Walker, *Mary Edwards Walker,* 158.

10. Howard, *In and Out,* 44, 47-48.

Chapter 15

1. *O.R.*, ser. 1, vol. 38, pt. 5, 409, 452.

2. Milo M. Quaife, ed., *From the Cannon's Mouth: The Civil War Letters of General Alpheus S. Williams* (Detroit: Wayne State University Press, 1959), 335-36.

3. A. A. Hoehling, *Last Train from Atlanta* (New York: Thomas Yoseloff, 1958), 213, 238-39, 263-64.

4. *O.R.*, ser. 1, vol. 38, pt. 5, 408-9, 419.

5. James Lee McDonough and James Pickett Jones, *War So Terrible: Sherman and Atlanta* (New York: W. W. Norton & Company, 1987), 269, 275.

6. Hoehling, *Last Train,* 362.

7. McDonough, *War So Terrible,* 271.

8. Hoehling, *Last Train,* 354.

9. McDonough, *War So Terrible,* 271, 275.

10. Hoehling, *Last Train,* 277, 317.

11. Robert G. Athearn, "An Indiana Doctor Marches with Sherman: The Diary of James Comfort Patten," *Indiana Magazine of History* 49, no. 4 (December 1953): 410.

12. *Memoirs of General William T. Sherman,* vol. 2 (Bloomington: Indiana University Press, 1957), 120.

Chapter 16

1. Hoehling, *Last Train,* 455.

2. *O.R.*, ser. 1, vol. 27, pt. 2, 140-41.

3. John Y. Simon, ed., *The Papers of Ulysses S. Grant* (Carbondale: Southern Illinois University Press, 1967), vol. 5, 238 and vol. 7, 50.

4. *Memoirs of General William T. Sherman,* 118; Hoehling, *Last Train,* 456.

5. *O.R.,* ser. 1, vol. 24, pt. 2, 356; *Memoirs of General William T. Sherman,* 118-20, 122, 124-26, 128.

6. Franklin M. Garrett, *Atlanta and Environs: A Chronicle of Its People and Events,* vol. 1 (Athens: University of Georgia Press, 1982), 642.

7. Hoehling, *Last Train,* 468-69.

8. John M. Gibson, *Those 163 Days* (New York: Bramhall House, 1961), 21-23.

9. Athearn, "An Indiana Doctor," 412-13.

10. Gibson, *Days,* 23.

11. Hoehling, *Last Train,* 455; Garrett, *Atlanta,* 643; John T. Trowbridge, *The Desolate South 1865-1866: A Picture of the Battlefields and of the Devastated Confederacy,* ed. Gordon Carroll (New York: Duell, Sloan and Pearce, 1956), 238; Gibson, *Days,* 29.

Chapter 17

1. John Scott, *Partisan Life with Col. John S. Mosby* (New York: Harper & Brothers, 1867), 227.

2. Cecil D. Eby, Jr., ed., *A Virginia Yankee in the Civil War: The Diaries of David Hunter Strother* (Chapel Hill: University of North Carolina Press, 1961), 235-36.

3. Scott, *Partisan Life,* 229.

4. Eby, *Virginia Yankee,* 237.

5. Ibid., 241.

6. Scott, *Partisan Life,* 228-29.

7. Eby, *Virginia Yankee,* 241.

8. Marshall Moore Brice, *Conquest of a Valley* (Verona, Va.: McClure Press, 1974), 100, 104-5, 107, 124.

9. *Staunton Vindicator,* 8 July 1864.

10. Ibid.; Brice, *Conquest,* 115.

11. Gary C. Walker, *Hunter's Fiery Raid through Virginia Valleys* (Roanoke, Va.: A&W Enterprise, 1989), 204; Brice, *Conquest,* 116.

12. *O.R.,* ser. 1, vol. 37, pt. 1, 97.

13. Eby, *Virginia Yankee,* 256.

14. Ibid., 262-63, 269-70.

15. Brice, *Conquest,* 131.

16. Eby, *Virginia Yankee,* 263.

17. Brice, *Conquest,* 131.

18. *O.R.,* ser. 1, vol. 37, pt. 2, 592.

19. Jubal A. Early, *A Memoir of the Last Year of the War for Independence in the Confederate States of America* (Columbia: University of South Carolina Press, 2001), 72, 74; Charles C. Osborne, *Jubal: The Life and Times of General Jubal A. Early, C.S.A., Defender of the Lost Cause* (Chapel Hill, N.C.: Algonquin Books, 1992), 268, 302, 304, 306.

20. *Staunton Vindicator,* 8 July 1864.

Chapter 18

1. *Staunton Vindicator,* 21 October 1864.

2. *O.R.,* ser. 2, vol. 43, pt. 2, 698.

3. Ibid., 202.

4. Jeffry D. Wert, *From Winchester to Cedar Creek: The Shenandoah Campaign of 1864* (Carlisle, Pa.: South Mountain Press, 1987), 159.

5. Thomas A. Ashby, *The Valley Campaigns* (New York: The Neale Publishing Co., 1914), 293; Virgil Carrington Jones, *Ranger Mosby* (Chapel Hill: University of North Carolina Press, 1944), 209-10.

6. "Hanging of Mosby's Men in 1864," *Southern Historical Society Papers* 24 (January 1896): 109.

7. J. H. Kidd, *Riding with Custer: Recollections of a Cavalryman in the Civil War* (Lincoln: University of Nebraska Press, 1997), 398-99.

8. George E. Pond, *The Shenandoah Valley in 1864* (New York: Charles Scribner's Sons, 1883), 192.

9. Kidd, *Custer,* 399-400.

10. Aldace F. Walker, *The Vermont Brigade in the Shenandoah Valley, 1864* (Burlington, Vt.: The Free Press Association, 1869), 128-29.

11. Richard R. Duncan, ed., *Alexander Neil and the Last Shenandoah Valley Campaign: Letters of an Army Surgeon to his Family, 1864* (Shippensburg, Pa.: White Mane Publishing Co., Inc., 1996), 68.

12. Samuel Horst, *Mennonites in the Confederacy: A Study in Civil War Pacifism* (Scottsdale, Pa.: Herald Press, 1967), 17, 102-3, 105.

13. Wert, *Shenandoah Campaign,* 145; Thomas F. Wildes, *Record of the One Hundred and Sixteenth Regiment Ohio Infantry Volunteers in the War of the Rebellion* (Sandusky, Ohio: I.F. Mack & Bro., Printers, 1884), 190; John W. Wayland, *Virginia Valley Records: Genealogical and Historical Materials of Rockingham County, Virginia and Related Regions* (Baltimore: Genealogical Publishing Co., Inc., 1978), 188-89.

14. Louis N. Boudrye, *Historic Records of the Fifth New York Cavalry* (Albany, N.Y.: S.R. Gray, 1865), 176.

15. Horst, *Mennonites,* 101-2.

16. Frank M. Myers, *The Comanches: A History of White's Battalion, Virginia Cavalry* (Baltimore: Kelly, Piet & Co., Publishers, 1871), 335-36.

17. John Scott, *Partisan Life with Col. John S. Mosby* (New York: Harper & Brothers, 1867), 376.

18. Ibid., 281-82.

19. *O.R.,* ser. 1, vol. 43, pt. 2, 308.

20. *Staunton Vindicator,* 21 October 1864.

Chapter 19

1. A. A. Hoehling, *Last Train from Atlanta* (New York: Thomas Yoseloff, 1958), 529.

2. *O.R.,* ser. 1, vol. 44, 8, 56.

3. Hoehling, *Last Train,* 522-24, 529.

4. Richard Harwell and Philip N. Racine, eds., *The Fiery Trail: A Union Officer's Account of Sherman's Last Campaigns* (Knoxville: University of Tennessee Press, 1986), 52.

5. Hoehling, *Last Train,* 531, 533, 537; E. R. Carter, *The Black Side: A Partial History of the Business, Religious and*

Educational Side of the Negro in Atlanta, Ga. (Atlanta: n.p., 1894), 14-15.

6. W. C. Johnson, "The March to the Sea," in *The Atlanta Papers,* comp. Sydney C. Kerksis (Dayton, Ohio: Morningside Bookshop, 1980), 809.

7. Hoehling, *Last Train,* 533-34.

8. Robert G. Athearn, "An Indiana Doctor Marches with Sherman: The Diary of James Comfort Patten," *Indiana Magazine of History* 49, no. 4 (December 1953): 417.

9. Franklin M. Garrett, *Atlanta and Environs: A Chronicle of Its People and Events* (Athens: University of Georgia Press, 1982), 655, 658.

10. Hoehling, *Last Train,* 538.

Chapter 20

1. *O.R.*, ser. 1, vol. 30, pt. 3, 697-98.

2. *Report of Major General William T. Sherman* (Millwood, N.Y.: Kraus Reprint Co., 1977), 236, 256.

3. Charles W. Wills, *Army Life of an Illinois Soldier,* comp. Mary E. Kellogg (Carbondale: Southern Illinois University Press, 1996), 313.

4. James A. Padgett, ed., "With Sherman Through Georgia and the Carolinas: Letters of a Federal Soldier," *Georgia Historical Quarterly* 33, no. 1 (March 1949): 49.

5. *Born in Slavery: Slave Narratives from the Federal Writers' Project, 1936-1938,* Georgia, vol. 4, pt. 1, 275. Library of Congress Web site: http://memory.loc.gov/ammen/snhtml/snhome.html. All quotations recorded in dialect have been rendered here in standard English.

6. *Memoirs of General William T. Sherman,* vol. 2 (Bloomington: Indiana University Press, 1957), 179-80.

7. James I. Robertson, Jr., ed., *The Diary of Dolly Lunt Burge* (Athens: University of Georgia Press, 1962), 93.

8. John M. Gibson, *Those 163 Days* (New York: Bramhall House, 1961), 39-40.

9. *Slave Narratives,* Georgia, vol. 4, pt. 3, 274, 276-77.

10. *Slave Narratives,* Georgia, vol. 4, pt. 2, 282-83.

11. *Slave Narratives,* Georgia, vol. 4, pt. 2, 278-79.

12. *Slave Narratives,* Georgia, vol. 4, pt. 1, 161, 167.

13. *Slave Narratives,* Georgia, vol. 4, pt. 1, 239, 248.

14. *Slave Narratives,* Georgia, vol. 4, pt. 3, 247, 255-56.

15. John T. Trowbridge, *The Desolate South 1865-1866: A Picture of the Battlefields and of the Devastated Confederacy,* ed. Gordon Carroll (New York: Duell, Sloan and Pearce, 1956), 259-60.

16. Louise Carolina Reese Cornwell, "General Howard Came at Tea Time," in Katharine M. Jones, *When Sherman Came: Southern Women and the "Great March,"* (Indianapolis: Bobbs-Merrill Company, 1964), 20.

17. Burke Davis, *Sherman's March* (New York: Random House, 1980), 66.

18. Gibson, *Days,* 46-47; *O.R.,* ser. 1, vol. 34, pt. 3, 713.

19. Gibson, *Days,* 56.

20. *Columbia Daily South Carolinian,* 2 December 1864.

21. Nora M. Canning, "General Slocum's Headquarters Were a Short Distance from the House," in Jones, *Sherman,* 52-54, 57.

22. Gibson, *Days,* 84.

23. Cornelia E. Screven, "The Army Encamped at Midway Church," in Jones, *Sherman,* 73.

24. Davis, *March,* 99.

25. Eliza Frances Andrews, *The War-Time Journal of a Georgia Girl 1864-1865,* ed. Spencer Bidwell King, Jr. (Macon, Ga.: The Ardivan Press, 1960), 32, 38.

26. Gibson, *Days,* 83.

27. Wills, *Army Life,* 326.

28. Gibson, *Days,* 60.

29. Ibid., 85.

30. Padgett, "With Sherman," 57-58.

31. Gibson, *Days,* 84.

32. Ibid., 85.

33. Ibid., 74.

34. *O.R.,* ser. 1, vol. 47, pt. 2, 36-37.

35. William T. Sherman to William M. McPherson, ca. 8 September 1864 (Sherman Papers, Huntington Library).

36. Richard Harwell and Philip N. Racine, eds., *The Fiery*

Trail: A Union Officer's Account of Sherman's Last Campaigns (Knoxville: University of Tennessee Press, 1986), 35, 47.

37. Gibson, *Days,* 113.

38. *Memoirs of General William T. Sherman,* 182-83.

Chapter 21

1. *O.R.,* ser. 1, vol. 44, 743.

2. Ibid., 799.

3. John Herr to his sister, 5 February 1865 (Special Collections Library, Duke University).

4. John K. Mahon, ed., "The Civil War Letters of Samuel Mahon, Seventh Iowa Infantry," *Iowa Journal of History* 51 (July 1953): 258, 262.

5. Nora M. Canning, "General Slocum's Headquarters Were a Short Distance from the House," in Jones, *Sherman,* 57.

6. Harwell, *Fiery Trail,* 102.

7. Edward G. Longacre, ed., "'We Left a Black Track in South Carolina': Letters of Corporal Eli S. Ricker, 1865," *South Carolina Historical Magazine* 82, no. 3 (July 1981): 215.

8. Burke Davis, *Sherman's March* (New York: Random House, 1980), 145-46.

9. Nancy Bostick DeSaussure, "Sherman's Army Was Crossing Savannah River," in Jones, *Sherman,* 112.

10. Gibson, *Days,* 146.

11. Oscar L. Jackson, *The Colonel's Diary* (Sharon, Pa.: privately published, 1922), 192.

12. Margaret Crawford Adams, "Army in Winnsboro . . . A Horrible Nightmare," in Jones, *Sherman,* 222.

13. Mrs. E. A. Steele, "Sherman's Fire Fiends," in Jones, *Sherman,* 133.

14. John T. Trowbridge, *The Desolate South 1865-1866: A Picture of the Battlefields and of the Devastated Confederacy,* ed. Gordon Carroll (New York: Duell, Sloan and Pearce, 1956), 303.

15. Mrs. Alfred Proctor Aldrich, "Barbarians in Barnwell," in Jones, *Sherman,* 120.

16. Mrs. "S.B.," "We Were Surprised by the Civility of their Manner," in Jones, *Sherman,* 130-31.

17. Sarah Jane Graham Sams, "I Felt as if the Lower Regions Had Been Turned Inside Out," in Jones, *Sherman,* 128.

18. Davis, *March,* 149; Gasper Loren Toole, II, *Ninety Years in Aiken County: Memoirs of Aiken County and Its People* (Charleston: Walker Evans & Cogswell, 1958), 357.

19. Harwell, *Fiery Trail,* 122.

20. James A. Padgett, ed., "With Sherman Through Georgia and the Carolinas: Letters of a Federal Soldier," *The Georgia Historical Quarterly* 53, no. 1 (March 1949): 72.

21. Janet Correll Ellison, ed., *On to Atlanta: The Civil War Diaries of John Hill Ferguson, Illinois Tenth Regiment of Volunteers* (Lincoln: University of Nebraska Press, 2001), 102, 108.

22. Davis, *March,* 151-52.

23. George Ward Nichols, *The Story of the Great March from the Diary of a Staff Officer* (New York: Harper & Brothers, Publishers, 1865), 207.

24. Mary A. McMichael, "Recollections of Sherman's Raid," in South Carolina Division United Daughters of the Confederacy, *Recollections and Reminiscences 1861-1865 through World War I,* vol. 4 (n.p.: United Daughters of the Confederacy, 1990-2000), 267.

25. Bessie C. Stribling, "Touching Loyalty—A Reminiscence of Mrs. Mary Bellinger Fishburne," in UDC, *Recollections,* vol. 4, 227.

26. Gibson, *Days,* 141.

27. Mrs. Orrie Sease Quattlebaum, "In Sherman's Wake," in UDC, *Recollections,* vol. 1, 646-47.

28. *Born in Slavery: Slave Narratives from the Federal Writers' Project, 1936-1938,* South Carolina, vol. 14, pt. 2, 209-11. Library of Congress Web site: http://memory.loc.gov/ammem/snhtml/snhome.html. All quotations recorded in dialect have been rendered here in standard English.

29. *Slave Narratives,* South Carolina, vol. 14, pt. 1, 75, 77.

30. Ellison, *Atlanta,* 105.

31. *Memoirs of General William T. Sherman,* 275.

32. H. W. Halleck, *Elements of International Law and Laws of War* (Philadelphia: J.B. Lippincott & Co., 1866), 198-99.

33. Anonymous Girl, "The Streets Were Filled with Homeless Families," in Jones, *Sherman,* 224-25.

34. Gibson, *Days,* 172.

35. Adams, "Nightmare," in Jones, *Sherman,* 222.

36. *Slave Narratives,* South Carolina, vol. 14, pt. 1, 51, 53.

37. *Slave Narratives,* South Carolina, vol. 14, pt. 3, 1, 3.

38. *Slave Narratives,* South Carolina, vol. 14, pt. 2, 242-43.

39. Miss Lutie Durham, "Incidents of Sherman's Raid in Fairfield County," in UDC, *Recollections,* vol. 3, 261, 263-64.

40. Mary Elinor Bouknight Poppenheim, "Burning Houses Light Their March," in Jones, *Sherman,* 244.

41. Anonymous Mother, "General Atkins and Staff," in Jones, *Sherman,* 236-37.

42. Esther Alden [Elizabeth Allston], "Their Triumphant Yells and Oaths," in Jones, *Sherman,* 250, 255.

43. Gibson, *Days,* 183-84.

44. Adams, "Nightmare," in Jones, *Sherman,* 223.

45. Julia Frances Gott, "They Whipped Mrs. R.," in Jones, *Sherman,* 229-30.

46. Davis, *March,* 186-87; Joseph T. Glatthaar, *The March to the Sea and Beyond: Sherman's Troops in the Savannah and Carolinas Campaign* (New York: New York University Press, 1985), 73-74.

47. *O.R.,* ser. 1, vol. 47, pt. 2, 546, 596-97.

48. Harwell, *Fiery Trail,* 153, 201.

49. Charles W. Wills, *Army Life of an Illinois Soldier,* ed. Mary E. Kellogg (Carbondale: Southern Illinois University Press, 1996), 342.

50. Jackson, *Diary,* 191.

51. Letter of Union private, 28 March 1865 (Clinton H. Haskell Collection, William L. Clements Library, University of Michigan).

52. Gibson, *Days,* 140.

Chapter 22

1. Harriott H. Ravenel, "An Endless Blue Column," in Jones,

Sherman, 157; O. M. Poe to Nellie, 26 December 1864 (O. M. Poe Papers, Library of Congress).

2. Tom Elmore, "The Burning of Columbia, South Carolina, February 17, 1865," *Blue & Gray Magazine* 21, no. 2 (winter 2004): 14.

3. *Memoirs of General William T. Sherman,* 278.

4. J. F. Williams, *Old and New Columbia* (Columbia: Epworth Orphanage Press, 1929), 120-21.

5. William Gilmore Simms, *Sack and Destruction of the City of Columbia, S.C.,* ed. A. S. Salley (Atlanta: Oglethorpe University Press, 1937), 33.

6. Elmore, "Burning of Columbia," 14.

7. Simms, *Sack and Destruction,* 35-36.

8. Elmore, "Burning of Columbia," 14, 16, 20-21.

9. Simms, *Sack and Destruction,* 40, 45, 47-48.

10. Ravenel, "Blue Column," 162.

11. William Gilmore Simms, *A City Laid Waste: The Capture, Sack, and Destruction of the City of Columbia,* ed. David Aiken (Columbia: University of South Carolina Press, 2005), 76; August Conrad, *The Destruction of Columbia, S.C.* (Columbia: The Wade Hampton Chapter of the United Daughters of the Confederacy, 1926), 28.

12. Simms, *Sack and Destruction,* 56.

13. John T. Trowbridge, *The Desolate South 1865-1866: A Picture of the Battlefields and of the Devastated Confederacy,* ed. Gordon Carroll (New York: Duell, Sloan and Pearce, 1956), 303.

14. Ibid., 302.

15. Simms, *Sack and Destruction,* 39.

16. Ibid., 48; Simms, *City Laid Waste,* 86.

17. Sophie Sosnowski, "It Was a Terrible Night," in Jones, *Sherman,* 174.

18. Ravenel, "Blue Column," 160.

19. William A. Nicholson, "The Burning of Columbia," in South Carolina Division United Daughters of the Confederacy, *Recollections and Reminiscences 1861-1865 through World War I,* vol. 6 (n.p.: United Daughters of the Confederacy, 1990-2000), 326.

20. Ravenel, "Blue Column," 160.

21. Anonymous Mother, "Sherman's Tigers," in Jones, *Sherman*, 176.

22. Emma Florence LeConte, "A Night of Horror," in Jones, *Sherman*, 181.

23. Lily Logan, "Demons in Human Shape," in Jones, *Sherman*, 164.

24. Eleanor Cohen, "The Burning of Columbia: Extract from a War Diary," in UDC, *Recollections*, vol. 4, 520.

25. Mary Rowe, "Sherman's Demons," in Jones, *Sherman*, 166; John M. Gibson, *Those 163 Days* (New York: Bramhall House, 1961), 161-62.

26. Mrs. "E.L.L.," "The Men Danced in the Streets," in Jones, *Sherman*, 169.

27. Agnes Law, "The Burning of Columbia—Affidavit of Mrs. Agnes Law," *Southern Historical Society Papers* 12 (1884): 233-34.

28. Nell S. Graydon, *Tales of Columbia* (Columbia: R.L. Bryan Co., 1964), 134; Gibson, *Days*, 164.

29. Sara Aldrich, "The Burning of the Ursuline Convent," in Jones, *Sherman*, 186.

30. Edwin J. Scott, *Random Recollections of a Long Life, 1806 to 1876* (Columbia: Charles A. Calvo Jr., printer, 1884), 183-84; Simms, *Sack and Destruction*, 87-89.

31. William Baugh to parents, 14 March and 27 March 1865 (William G. Baugh collection, Robert W. Woodruff Library, Emory University).

32. Scott, *Random Recollections*, 183-84.

33. Rachel Sherman Thorndike, ed., *The Sherman Letters: Correspondence Between General and Senator Sherman from 1837 to 1891* (New York: Charles Scribner's Sons, 1894), 266.

34. *Memoirs of General William T. Sherman*, 287-88.

35. Allan D. Charles, "The Burning of Columbia," *Southern Partisan* 1, no. 34 (spring/summer 1981): 9.

36. John Hammond Moore, *Columbia and Richland County: A South Carolina Community, 1740-1900* (Columbia: University of South Carolina Press, 1993), 203, 208. Emphasis in the original.

37. Marion Brunson Lucas, *Sherman and the Burning of Columbia* (College Station: Texas A&M University Press, 1976).

38. J. F. Carrol, "The Burning of Columbia, South Carolina—

Report of the Committee of Citizens Appointed to Collect Testimony," *Southern Historical Society Papers* 8 (1880): 212-14.

Chapter 23

1. Burke Davis, *Sherman's March* (New York: Random House, 1980), 209.

2. Walter Brian Cisco, *Taking a Stand: Portraits from the Southern Secession Movement* (Shippensburg, Pa.: White Mane Books, 1998), 109, 111.

3. Alan C. Downs, "North Carolina," in Archie P. McDonald, ed., *A Nation of Sovereign States: Secession & War in the Confederacy* (Murfreesboro, Tenn.: Southern Heritage Press, 1994), 133; Thomas L. Livermore, *Numbers & Losses in the Civil War in America 1861-65* (Carlisle, Pa.: John Kallmann, Publishers, 1996), 23.

4. M. A. De Wolfe, ed., *Home Letters of General Sherman* (New York: Charles Scribner's Sons, 1909), 342.

5. Cornelia Phillips Spencer, *The Last Ninety Days of the War in North Carolina* (New York: Watchman Publishing Company, 1866), 62, 64.

6. John M. Gibson, *Those 163 Days* (New York: Bramhall House, 1961), 189-90.

7. Esther Alden, "Nothing but Creatures and Human Beings in Agony," in Jones, *Sherman,* 262.

8. Gibson, *Days,* 216.

9. Davis, *March,* 222.

10. Gibson, *Days,* 204.

11. A Woman of Fayetteville, "Terrible Has Been the Storm," in Jones, *Sherman,* 285-86.

12. Josephine Bryan Worth, "Sherman's Raid," in UDC, *Recollections,* vol. 4, 298.

13. James A. Padgett, ed., "With Sherman Through Georgia and the Carolinas: Letters of a Federal Soldier," *The Georgia Historical Quarterly* 53, no. 1 (March 1949): 74.

14. Alice Campbell, "The Nights Were Made Hideous with Smoke," in Jones, *Sherman,* 274.

15. Sally Hawthorne, "What Did General Sherman Say," in Jones, *Sherman,* 284.

16. Ibid., 280.

17. Spencer, *Last Ninety Days,* 68.

18. Georgia Hicks, "These Ruffians," in Jones, *Sherman,* 296-97.

19. Clara D. Maclean, "The Horrible Comedy Ended," in Jones, *Sherman* 314-15.

20. Cornelia Phillips Spencer, "For Thirty-six Hours They Poured into Goldsboro," in Jones, *Sherman,* 291.

21. Oscar L. Jackson, *The Colonel's Diary* (Sharon, Pa.: privately published, 1922), 208.

22. Janet Correll Ellison, ed., *On to Atlanta: The Civil War Diaries of John Hill Ferguson, Illinois Tenth Regiment of Volunteers* (Lincoln: University of Nebraska Press, 2001), 122.

Chapter 24

1. David C. Edmonds, ed., *The Conduct of Federal Troops in Louisiana During the Invasions of 1863 and 1864: Official Report Compiled from Sworn Testimony Under Direction of Governor Henry W. Allen, Shreveport, April 1865* (Lafayette, La.: Acadiana Press, 1988), 168-70.

2. David C. Edmonds, *Yankee Autumn in Acadiana* (Lafayette, La.: Acadiana Press, 1979), 61-62, 242.

3. Edmonds, ed., *Conduct,* 138-40.

4. Ibid., 115-21, 202; Edmonds, *Autumn,* 139, 147.

5. Susan Dabney Smedes, *Memorials of a Southern Planter* (Baltimore: Cushings & Bailey, 1888), 210; Journal entry 14 August 1862 (Journal of James Andrew Agnew, typescript in author's possession).

6. William T. Sherman to John Sherman, 26 April 1863 (William T. Sherman Papers, Library of Congress); Walter T. Durham, *Nashville, the Occupied City* (Nashville: The Tennessee Historical Society, 1985), 182-83; Stephen V. Ash, *Middle Tennessee Society Transformed, 1860-1870: War and Peace in the Upper South* (Baton Rouge: Louisiana State University Press, 1988), 107-8, 133-34.

7. Edmund L. Drago, "How Sherman's March Through

Georgia Affected the Slaves," *Georgia Historical Quarterly* 57, no. 3 (fall 1973): 370-71.

8. Mary Sharpe Jones and Mary Jones Mallard, *Yankees A' Coming: One Month's Experience During the Invasion of Liberty County, Georgia, 1864-1865,* ed. Haskell Monroe (Tuscaloosa, Ala.: Confederate Publishing Company, Inc., 1959), 52; Drago, "Slaves," 371.

9. Frances Thomas Howard, *In and Out of the Lines: An Accurate Account of Incidents During the Occupation of Georgia by Federal Troops in 1864-65* (Cartersville, Ga.: Etowah Valley Historical Society, 1998), 15-16. All quotations recorded in dialect have been rendered here in standard English.

10. *Born in Slavery: Slave Narratives from the Federal Writers' Project, 1936-1938,* Georgia, vol. 4, pt. 1, 313. Library of Congress Web site: http://memory.loc.gov/ammem/snhtml/snhome.html.

11. *Slave Narratives,* Georgia, vol. 4, pt. 2, 295, 298.

12. James I. Robertson, Jr., ed., *The Diary of Dolly Lunt Burge* (Athens: University of Georgia Press, 1962), 102.

13. Allie Travis, "A Moving Mass of Blue Coats," in Jones, *Sherman,* 7.

14. Nora M. Canning, "General Slocum's Headquarters Were a Short Distance from the House," in Jones, *Sherman,* 58-59.

15. Mrs. Alfred Proctor Aldrich, "Barbarians in Barnwell," in Jones, *Sherman,* 116.

16. Florence Maria Henerey, "Slave Loyalty," in UDC, *Recollections,* vol. 3, 465-6.

17. *Slave Narratives,* South Carolina, vol. 14, pt. 2, 203, 205.

18. *Slave Narratives,* South Carolina, vol. 14, pt. 4, 5.

19. *Slave Narratives,* South Carolina, vol. 14, pt. 3, 167, 170.

20. *Slave Narratives,* South Carolina, vol. 14, pt. 3, 195.

21. *Slave Narratives,* South Carolina, vol. 14, pt. 4, 266-68.

22. *Slave Narratives,* South Carolina, vol. 14, pt. 2, 335-36.

23. Minnie Mulloy Rice, "One of the Faithful—A Negro Slave Nurse," in UDC, *Recollections,* vol. 4, 451-52.

24. *Slave Narratives,* South Carolina, vol. 14, pt. 2, 32.

25. Anna Hasell Thomas, "The Entire Neighborhood Was on Fire," in Jones, *Sherman,* 211, 216.

26. Oscar L. Jackson, *The Colonel's Diary* (Sharon, Pa.: privately published, 1922), 194.

27. *Slave Narratives,* South Carolina, vol. 14, pt. 2, 216-17.

28. Sophie Sosnowski, "Sherman . . . Showed Great Temper," in Jones, *Sherman,* 194.

29. Sophie Sosnowski, "It Was a Terrible Night," in Jones, *Sherman,* 174-75.

30. William Gilmore Simms, *A City Laid Waste: The Capture, Sack, and Destruction of the City of Columbia* ed. David Aiken (Columbia: University of South Carolina Press, 2005), 90.

31. Ibid., 108.

32. Jackson, *Diary,* 193.

33. Mary Chesnut, *The Private Mary Chesnut: The Unpublished Civil War Diaries,* ed. C. Vann Woodward and Elisabeth Muhlenfeld (New York: Oxford University Press, 1984), 242. The editor of *Mary Chesnut's Civil War,* C. Vann Woodward, dismisses this bayoneting incident as "an unfounded rumor" (810). Mrs. Chesnut was sufficiently convinced of its veracity to include it in both her private diary and the work she later published.

34. John M. Gibson, *Those 163 Days* (New York: Bramhall House, 1961), 204-5, 253.

35. *Slave Narratives,* North Carolina, vol. 11, pt. 2, 268.

36. Cornelia Phillips Spencer, "They Took Quiet Possession of Raleigh," in Jones, *Sherman,* 299.

37. *Slave Narratives,* North Carolina, vol. 11, pt. 1, 255-56.

38. *Slave Narratives,* North Carolina, vol. 11, pt. 1, 65.

39. *Slave Narratives,* North Carolina, vol. 11, pt. 1, 9, 10-12.

40. *Slave Narratives,* South Carolina, vol. 14, pt. 3, 23, 26.

Index

215